A Lifetime of
GOOD EATS

The Foods I Love to Cook and Share

always have fun in the kitchen !

Holly

Holly Amidon

LifeRich Publishing is a registered trademark of The Reader's Digest Association, Inc.

LifeRich Publishing books may be ordered through booksellers or by contacting:

LifeRich Publishing
1663 Liberty Drive
Bloomington, IN 47403
www.liferichpublishing.com
1 (888) 238-8637

Because of the dynamic nature of the Internet, any web addresses or links contained in this book may have changed since publication and may no longer be valid. The views expressed in this work are solely those of the author and do not necessarily reflect the views of the publisher, and the publisher hereby disclaims any responsibility for them.

Photographs by Karen Barnes

Any people depicted in stock imagery provided by Thinkstock are models, and such images are being used for illustrative purposes only. Certain stock imagery © Thinkstock.

ISBN: 978-1-4897-0932-5 (sc)
ISBN: 978-1-4897-0933-2 (hc)
ISBN: 978-1-4897-0931-8 (e)

Library of Congress Control Number: 2016917730

Print information available on the last page.

LifeRich Publishing rev. date: 10/31/2016

I dedicate this book to my husband, Joel. Although he has no passion for cooking, he has always said that it is just as important to have a passion for eating! He is my biggest fan, complimenting my every effort no matter how extravagant or simple, tasty or not so much.

Contents

Preface

I have always loved food…preparing it, sharing it, and eating it! I feel so blessed to have had a food rich upbringing with many mentors and patient teachers who encouraged me to experiment and be creative in the kitchen. When I was about eleven or so, I clearly remember planning an anniversary dinner for my parents. I wish I still had the crayon written menu, but I know it boasted of pastry wrapped green olives as an appetizer, a homemade crust pizza, and a fresh tossed salad. I set the kitchen table with a red and white checkered cloth, lit a candle, and voilà, a romantic dinner for two!

My favorite cooking guides of my youth were the **Nancy Drew Cookbook** and the ever-popular **Betty Crocker Cookbook,** which still holds a prominent spot in my kitchen cubby. My dad loves to cook as well, and he has added to my book collection several times. Most notably, when I got married 31 years ago he presented me with Julia Child's **Mastering the Art of French Cooking, Volume Two**. It is well worn and dog-eared, but interestingly enough I have only read it. I did not attempt to try any of her recipes until recently as I think I have been intimidated! A few years back Dad gave me another cookbook gift called **Intercourses, an aphrodisiac cookbook**. Now **that** one I have used! What fun it has been to plan dinner parties for our gourmet group around that theme. Many of my friends and my brother, Chris, have asked to borrow it several times.

Recently my daughter, Paige, has shown an interest in learning how to wow friends with delicious dishes. She calls for ideas and advice, and I am thrilled to help. The same goes for my son, Joel Rhein, who throughout the years has enjoyed cooking not only for himself, but also for roommates and friends. One Christmas a few years back I put together recipe boxes for both of them…similar yet different, based on their personal tastes and most requested recipes. I enjoyed sifting through my myriads of handwritten and torn out of magazines recipes and picking out their favorites to add to their culinary repertoire. Nothing super hard or über fancy. Just the comfort foods of their growing up years. My Nana did the same for me *when I was a new bride. I still treasure that beautifully written book in her perfect Palmer Method script.*

*I create my dishes in a variety of ways. Sometimes I thumb through my many cookbooks and pull an appetizer from this one and a main dish from that one and slowly build up a complete meal. My monthly arrival of **bon appétit** magazine is another source of endless ideas and challenges. I have been known to get it in the morning mail, head to the grocery store for ingredients, and cook all afternoon so I can have a gourmet dinner on the table for my husband's arrival home. Sometimes I just open up the refrigerator and my cupboards, see what I have on hand, and make something up. Often I refer back to the collection of handwritten, not in any semblance of order, scraps of paper or recipe cards from my dear friends who are always kind enough to share their tried-and-true dishes. I feel that by exchanging and sharing these recipes we are expressing our love for those who have created culinary traditions in the past as well as respecting our fellow foodies of the present and trusting that our high standards will be preserved in the future. No matter how I go about it, the fact remains: I love to spend time in the kitchen!*

This book has been many years in the making, but it feels like just the right time to finally collect my favorite recipes together and share them. I hope you enjoy!

Joel Rhein · mini-me

Sweet Paige

Cooking with Mom

ana's Thanksgiving table

Chris's kitchen mischief

Teenage chef

Rise and Shine Breakfast Treats

Bran Muffins

Blueberry Coffeecake

Croissant Surprise

Sour Cream Coffee Cake

Pumpkin Chocolate Chip Muffins

Cinnamon Raisin Loaves

Eggs in Bacon Baskets

Egg and Sausage Casserole

Quiche Lorraine

Breakfast Pizza

Notes

Bran Muffins

This is a wonderful breakfast offering that I have made countless times over the past 30 years. The little pink slip of paper that I scribbled the recipe on when I was a young bride is stained and tattered. They are best fresh out of the oven, and I never feel guilty about eating more than one because they are so healthy…right??

1 cup boiling water
1 cup vegetable or canola oil
1 cup sugar
2 beaten eggs
2 ½ cups all-purpose flour
2 ½ teaspoons baking soda
½ teaspoon salt
1 cup wheat germ
1 cup *All-Bran* cereal
1 cup bran flakes
1 cup chopped dates
2 cups buttermilk

COMBINE the water, oil, sugar, and eggs in a large mixing bowl. Stir in the flour, soda, and salt, then add in the wheat germ, *All-Bran*, bran flakes, and dates. Mix well. Stir in the 2 cups of buttermilk, then place in greased muffin tins and bake for 20 minutes at 375°. Makes 24 muffins.

Blueberry Coffeecake

I believe my sister-in-law, Susan, got this recipe from her sister and then shared it with lucky me. This makes 2 loaves. I often freeze one so that I can pull it out when we make the long nighttime drive down to Emerald Isle, North Carolina. It is so nice to wake up by the ocean the next morning to a cup of coffee and this wonderful, sweet bread.

cake

4 cups all-purpose flour

1 ½ cups sugar

1 tablespoon plus 2 teaspoons baking powder

1 ½ teaspoons salt

1 stick unsalted butter, softened

1 ½ cups whole milk

2 eggs

4 cups fresh or frozen blueberries (fresh work better)

topping

1 cup sugar

2/3 cup all-purpose flour

1 teaspoon cinnamon

1 stick unsalted butter, softened

BEAT the first 7 ingredients together in a large mixing bowl for 30 seconds. Stir in the berries. Fill 2 greased loaf pans half full with the cake batter. Make the topping and sprinkle over the loaves. Bake for 55 to 60 minutes at 375°.

Croissant Surprise

Joel and I were feeling particularly entrepreneurial about 15 years ago when we decided to buy a rundown old building on a canal not too far from our home and turn it into an inn and restaurant. I guess we had some notion that running a B & B full time while still parenting two young children, maintaining other jobs, and living 20 minutes away was going to be easy and enjoyable. Add to that all the time, money, and effort it took to get La Mariposa up and functional and call us crazy! It was great fun to create, though, because all of our family and friends jumped right in to help us. For a while life was magical, but unfortunately the experience of daily operations was overwhelming, and eventually we had to sell. We have moved on from that venture, but the lessons learned were invaluable, and I am still preparing the breakfast dishes that I created for our guests. This is one of my favorites.

1 croissant per serving
1 egg per serving
¼ cup half and half per serving
Orange marmalade or any sweet preserve of your choosing
Orange juice
½ teaspoon vanilla extract per serving

GREASE a baking dish large enough to hold several croissants. Cut each croissant horizontally in half and smear the bottom half with a mixture of marmalade and just enough orange juice to make it easily spreadable. Top with the other croissant half and spread on more of the marmalade mixture. In a bowl, beat together the eggs, half and half, and vanilla. Pour over the croissants. Cover with plastic wrap and refrigerate overnight. Let stand at room temperature for about 30 minutes before baking, uncovered, at 375° for 35 to 40 minutes, or until golden brown.

Sour Cream Coffee Cake

This is a tasty treat that I have been making for years. It is also written on a worn out piece of pink paper. I usually make it on a Sunday morning because it makes the kitchen smell so good and sets the tone for a nice, relaxing day.

cake
¼ cup unsalted butter, softened
1 cup sugar
2 eggs
2 cups all-purpose flour
1 teaspoon baking soda
1 teaspoon baking powder
1 teaspoon vanilla extract
1 cup sour cream

topping
¼ cup packed brown sugar
1 teaspoon cinnamon

CREAM the butter and sugar in a large mixing bowl. Add in the eggs and beat well. In a separate bowl, sift together the flour, baking soda, and baking powder. Add these dry ingredients plus the sour cream and vanilla to the creamed butter, sugar, and eggs. Mix well. Place half of the batter into a greased bundt pan. Combine the brown sugar and cinnamon to make the topping. Sprinkle half of the topping onto the cake. Add the rest of the batter, then sprinkle with the remaining topping. Bake at 325° for 50 minutes.

Pumpkin Chocolate Chip Muffins

Hands down, this is the most requested food that I do! I started making these muffins when the kids were little, having wrangled the recipe from the school nurse when I was a new guidance counselor. Of course they are popular in the fall and into the holiday season, but I find they taste great any time of year. When Joel Rhein was studying in the islands and Paige had moved out to Southern California, they both missed the change of seasons and thus these autumnal treats. Rest assured, they each have the recipe in their hands now, and rumor has it they make them as frequently as I do!

2 cups sugar
½ cup vegetable or canola oil
3 eggs
1 ½ cups canned solid-pack pumpkin
½ cup water
3 cups all-purpose flour
1 ½ teaspoons baking powder
1 teaspoon baking soda
1 teaspoon salt
½ teaspoon ground cloves
¾ teaspoon cinnamon
½ teaspoon nutmeg
1 (6 ounce bag) semi-sweet chocolate chips

COMBINE the sugar, oil, eggs, pumpkin, and water in a large mixing bowl. Blend well. In a separate bowl, sift together the flour, baking powder, baking soda, salt, cloves, cinnamon, and nutmeg. Stir into the first mixture. Add in the chocolate chips. Grease 2 muffin tins and fill each cup with the pumpkin batter. Bake at 400° for about 15 minutes.

Cinnamon Raisin Loaves

I never attempted to bake my own homemade bread until fairly recently when our dear friend, Aliena, spent a weekend with us for a family gathering and convinced me that there are no smoke and mirrors involved. She and her family live in a remote, country town in rural Vermont. They homeschool their children and live an inspirational, wholesome life. Aliena wrote out her no-fail recipe during her visit and then sent me a beautiful artisan bread cookbook via Amazon. I couldn't have been more thrilled! This bread is wonderful as is or even better as French Toast. It makes enough dough for 2 loaves, so I often make one at a time and keep the second portion in the refrigerator for up to 5 days.

2 cups lukewarm water

1 cup buttermilk

1 tablespoon granulated yeast

1 tablespoon Kosher salt

1 ½ tablespoons sugar

6 ½ cups all-purpose flour

1/3 cup sugar

1 ½ teaspoons cinnamon

¾ cup golden raisins

1 egg and 2 teaspoons water for egg wash

STIR the first 5 ingredients together in the large bowl of a standing mixer until the yeast has dissolved. Mix in the flour with the paddle attachment. Loosely cover with plastic wrap and let sit at room temperature for approximately 2 hours. The dough can be used at this point, but it is easier to handle when chilled. Whether you chill the dough or not, when you are ready to bake the bread, lightly flour a cutting board and a rolling pin. Grease a loaf pan and set aside. Cut the dough in half, fashion one portion into a ball, then roll out to about an 8" by 16" rectangle. Mix the cinnamon and sugar together and spread evenly over the dough. Sprinkle on the raisins. Starting at the short end, roll up the dough, jelly-roll style, and tuck into the prepared pan. Cover with plastic wrap and let sit on the counter for 90 minutes. Preheat the oven to 375°. Beat the egg and water together to make the wash. Remove the plastic wrap and brush the loaf with the egg wash and bake for 40 minutes, or until golden brown.

Eggs in Bacon Baskets

Before our friends Ron and Fran built their house in Emerald Isle, North Carolina, 5 doors down from us, we would travel to the beach together on vacation and Fran would make us lovely breakfasts every morning. This was one of my favorites because of its delicious simplicity. I now like to make it for overnight guests and pair it with one of my coffeecake sweet treats.

12 strips thick bacon
12 eggs
½ to ¾ cup half and half

Paprika
Coarse ground black pepper
Salt to taste

COOK the bacon until almost done. Do not let it get crisp. Line each cup of a muffin tin with a bacon strip and break an egg into the hole. Top with 2 to 3 tablespoons of the half and half and sprinkle with paprika, pepper, and salt. Bake at 350° for 13 to 15 minutes. Gently remove from the tin and serve immediately.

Egg and Sausage Casserole

This is another recipe from my La Mariposa *days. It needs to be made ahead and refrigerated to let the bread soak up all the scrumptious flavors. I serve this to my out-of-town guests, at family brunches and holiday gatherings, and most recently at my brother-in-law's bistro when we cater private parties. Tom and I and the rest of the Kikko's staff really enjoy pooling all of our culinary talents and ideas into making these functions successful.*

6 pieces of sourdough bread
½ stick unsalted butter, softened
1 pound bulk sausage, sweet or medium
1 cup sharp cheddar cheese, shredded
6 eggs
2 cups whole milk
1 teaspoon dry mustard
Salt and pepper to taste

BUTTER each slice of bread, then cut into small pieces and place in a greased 13" by 9" baking dish. Brown the sausage and drain. Sprinkle over the bread. Top with the shredded cheddar cheese. Mix the eggs, milk, mustard, salt, and pepper in a bowl. Pour over the bread and sausage. Cover with plastic wrap and refrigerate overnight. When ready to cook, remove the plastic wrap, preheat the oven to 350°, and bake for 35 to 40 minutes.

Quiche Lorraine

The thing I love about quiche recipes is that you can add in almost any type of cheese, meat, or vegetable. The basics, eggs and cream, remain the same. When I have time, I try to make the crust the way my Nana taught my mom, who in turn taught me. Let's just say that I am not a natural at this like my foremothers were, so often I cheat and use a store-bought crust. I did have a big breakthrough a few years back, though, when my friend and neighbor in Emerald Isle invited me over for a pie crust tutorial. Korin makes wonderful berry pies, and I am grateful that she shared her secrets with me. This classic quiche is perfect for a brunch or luncheon.

3 eggs, lightly beaten
1 cup light cream
5 slices bacon, cooked and crumbled
¼ cup onion, finely chopped
1 cup Swiss cheese, grated
Salt and pepper to taste
1 unbaked 9 inch pie shell

MIX all 6 ingredients in a bowl and pour into the pie shell. Bake at 375° for 35 to 40 minutes.

Nana's Pie Crust

1 ¾ cups all-purpose flour
3 tablespoons *Crisco* shortening
Salt to taste
¼ cup cold water

PLACE the flour into a bowl and whisk in some salt. Mix the Crisco into the flour with a fork until crumbly. Slowly stir in the cold water until mixed. Knead into a ball. Either roll out right away or brush with flour and wrap tightly in plastic wrap and store in the refrigerator.

Breakfast Pizza

What a novel idea! Pizza anytime is fun, but nothing beats it as a morning meal. I make my own pizza dough, but I do find that the pre-portioned little balls that I can buy at the grocery store taste just as good and allow me to whip up a pizza pie at a moment's notice. As with my quiche recipe, you can use any toppings to complement the eggs.

pizza
6 eggs
¼ cup half and half
Salt and pepper to taste
Garlic powder
Fresh parsley, chopped
½ stick unsalted butter
2 cups Canadian bacon, cut into bite-size cubes
1 cup sharp cheddar cheese, shredded

1 cup mozzarella cheese, shredded
Parmesan cheese, grated
EVOO
Cornmeal

dough
7 ½ cups all-purpose flour
4 teaspoons salt
½ teaspoon yeast
3 cups lukewarm water

ALLOW yourself an overnight for the dough. First, whisk the flour, salt, and yeast together in a medium bowl. Gradually add in the water while stirring continuously with a wooden spoon. Mix the dough gently with your hands to form a rough ball. Transfer to a larger bowl and cover with plastic wrap. Let the dough rise at room temperature, away from any drafts, for at least 18 hours. The dough will double in size, and the surface will be covered with little bubbles. Lay the dough on a floured surface and shape into a rectangle. Divide into even portions of 6 or 7 and form into little balls. Leave on the floured surface and cover with a damp towel. Allow to rise for 1 more hour. Either use immediately or wrap each ball tightly in plastic wrap and refrigerate or freeze. If chilling, be sure to let the dough come back to room temperature before preparing the pizza.

Whisk together the eggs and the half and half. Add the salt, pepper, a dash of garlic powder, and the parsley. Melt the butter in a skillet and scramble the eggs over medium heat until almost done. Set aside. Prepare a pizza stone by lightly brushing it with EVOO and then spreading some cornmeal evenly across the surface. Work the dough onto the stone with your fingers, trying to stretch it all the way to the edges. Brush the dough with EVOO. Sprinkle on the cheddar cheese, then spread the eggs over the top. Next, top with the Canadian bacon, then the mozzarella and Parmesan cheeses. Bake in a 350° oven for 25 to 30 minutes. Remove from the oven and let sit for a minute before slicing.

Notes

Snacks and Apps

Macaroons

Caramel Corn

Biscotti

Katherine's Granola

Chicken Liver Pâté

Buffalo Chicken Wing Dip

Coconut Shrimp

Fried Polenta Squares with Anchovy Sauce

Garlic Escargots in Mushroom Caps

Seared Foie Gras with Cinnamon Raisin French Toast

Ground Pork and Vegetable Egg Rolls

Horned Dorset Hot Cheese Dip

Pimento Cheese Dip

Guacamole, Salsa Style

Rumaki (Bacon Wrapped Chicken Livers)

Shrimp Creole Appetizer

Notes

Macaroons

These are so easy to make! I love them with an afternoon cup of coffee. They are also a wonderful treat to package up nicely and give as gifts to friends.

1 stick unsalted butter, softened
¾ cup sugar
2 teaspoons finely grated orange or lemon peel

3 eggs
6 cups sweetened, flaked coconut
Chocolate syrup for drizzling

BEAT the butter and sugar until smooth. Add in the orange or lemon peel, then the eggs, one at a time, beating well after each addition. Stir in the coconut flakes. Spoon about a tablespoon and a half of the batter onto cookie sheets lined with parchment paper, trying to get 12 cookies per batch. Bake in a 325° oven, one sheet at a time, for approximately 25 minutes, or until the bottoms are golden brown. If you wish, drizzle a little chocolate sauce on each macaroon.

Caramel Corn

When I was a teenager I loved to go to the mall. Sometimes it was more about the eating than the shopping! A favorite guilty pleasure of mine was the sweet and salty combination of the caramel corn from the food court. I also liked to sample kettle corn at craft fairs and festivals. Now I make this decadent snack at home for special occasions and sometimes just because I crave it.

Corn for popping (about 12 cups when popped)
Vegetable or canola oil
1 ¼ sticks unsalted butter
1 ½ cups packed light brown sugar
½ cup corn syrup
½ teaspoon salt
1 ½ teaspoons vanilla extract
½ teaspoon baking soda

POP the corn in batches on the stove in a large pot of hot oil (with a lid!) and then place in a large greased aluminum roasting pan. Sprinkle on some salt and stir to evenly season. Melt the butter in a heavy saucepan over medium to high heat. Add the brown sugar, corn syrup, and salt and bring to a boil. Reduce the heat to medium and simmer, stirring occasionally, until slightly thickened, approximately 3 to 4 minutes. Remove from the heat and stir in the vanilla and baking soda. The mixture will bubble up. Pour over the popcorn and gently toss to coat. Bake in a 250° oven for about 1 and a half hours, stirring occasionally.

Biscotti

My friend, Theresa, shared this recipe when our kids were all back in elementary and middle school together. About once a month we would have each other over for coffee, sweets, and "mom" time. The kids lucked out because when they arrived home they got the leftovers! This is a fun cookie because the recipe allows you to add in whatever fruits or candies you prefer. You can also easily double it to serve large crowds.

1 stick unsalted butter, softened

¾ cup sugar

1 teaspoon vanilla extract

3 large eggs

1 ¾ cups all-purpose or wheat flour

1 cup cornmeal

1 ½ teaspoons baking powder

1 cup sweetened, flaked coconut

1 cup white chocolate chips

BEAT the butter and sugar with a hand mixer until smooth. Add the eggs and vanilla and beat until well blended, scraping down the sides of the bowl as needed. Combine the flour, cornmeal, and baking powder and beat into the butter mixture. Stir in the coconut flakes and white chocolate chips. Spoon 1 cup of the dough in dollops down the length of a greased baking sheet, 1 inch from the edge. Do the same on the other side of the baking sheet and repeat on another sheet. With floured fingers, pat each strip of dough into a flat 13 inch loaf, about ½ inch thick and 2 inches wide. Bake the loaves in a 350° oven until golden brown, approximately 15 to 20 minutes. Switch pans in the oven about halfway through to keep them baking evenly. Remove from the oven and cut the loaves crosswise into ½ inch thick slices. Separate the slices slightly and tip each onto a cut side. Return to the oven and bake until the cookies are slightly darker and firm and dry to the touch, about 15 to 20 minutes longer. Cool on racks.

Katherine's Granola

Our son's girlfriend, Katherine, is a whiz in the kitchen. She learned a lot from her Nonna who recently passed away. Whenever they come to visit she always digs right in to help me prep and cook whatever is on the menu. She has shared several of her favorite recipes with me. What I like about this one is you can swap in and out whatever seeds or dried fruits you desire and avoid the nuts, which I must do because of my allergies. This is a terrific snack sprinkled over yogurt or to bag up and take on a hike or a long bike ride.

4 cups rolled oats

1 cup unsweetened, flaked coconut

1 cup unsalted pumpkin seeds

½ cup *All-Bran* cereal

½ cup wheat germ

¼ cup flax seeds

1 tablespoon cinnamon

1 ½ teaspoons cardamom

½ teaspoon salt

1/3 cup EVOO

1/3 cup honey

¼ cup each of golden raisins, sweetened chopped dates, dried mango bits, chocolate chips

MIX all ingredients together except the dried fruit and chocolate chips in a large bowl. Add the EVOO and honey. Stir to combine and pour onto a non-greased cookie sheet. Bake at 300° for 40 minutes, stirring halfway through by pulling the outside edges of the granola to the middle and flattening back out. Bake until golden in color. Pour the granola into a large bowl and cool completely before adding the dried fruits and chocolate chips.

Chicken Liver Pâté

Our friend Phil from North Carolina shared this recipe with me several years ago. I prepare it as a starter when I am doing a gourmet meal as it seems so chic! Be sure to drain off the broth after cooking the livers. I forgot to do so the very first time and it just didn't set up right.

1 (20 ounce) container fresh chicken livers, undrained

1 cup chicken stock

¼ cup red onion, diced

Sprig of rosemary

6 or 7 strips of bacon cooked crisp then crumbled

½ stick unsalted butter, softened

½ teaspoon dry mustard

¼ teaspoon salt

¼ teaspoon fresh ground black pepper

1 ounce bourbon

SIMMER the chicken livers in their juices and the chicken broth with the onions and rosemary until cooked through, about 15 minutes. Remove the sprig of rosemary, cool, drain and reserve the broth.

Place about ¼ cup of the broth, livers and onions, and the rest of the ingredients in a blender. Run until smooth. Cover and chill overnight if possible. Sprinkle with fresh parsley and serve with crusty bread or delicate table crackers depending on the mood you are going for.

Buffalo Chicken Wing Dip

Who doesn't love chicken wing dip? There are certainly many variations of the recipe, but I model mine on my friend Joyce's and add a few twists and turns. Crazy good!

4 boneless, skinless chicken breasts
2 (8 ounce) bricks cream cheese
1 (12 ounce) bottle or jar Ranch dressing
¾ to nearly 1 cup hot sauce
1 (8 ounce) bag shredded sharp cheddar cheese

BOIL the chicken in lightly salted water until cooked through, approximately 15 minutes. Remove the chicken and place on a cutting board to cool a bit. Shred with a fork then place in an 8 ½" by 11" baking dish. Pour on the hot sauce and stir to combine. Cover with plastic wrap and refrigerate to allow the chicken to soak up the flavor of the hot sauce. When ready to cook, preheat the oven to 350°, take the chicken out of the refrigerator and remove the plastic wrap. Melt the cream cheese bricks over medium heat and pour in the Ranch dressing and stir until all mixed. Pour this mixture over the chicken. Bake for 10 minutes. Remove from the oven and sprinkle the shredded cheddar over the top. Return to the oven for 10 to 15 more minutes, or until the cheese is bubbly and starting to brown. Serve hot with celery and blue cheese dressing as well as a bowl of tortilla chips.

Coconut Shrimp

This is a bon appétit *recipe that I do for large family gatherings, typically around the Christmas holidays. Once, in an attempt to be healthier, I baked rather than fried the shrimp. The overwhelming response was to go back to frying, most emphatically from Paige!*

1 egg
½ cup all-purpose flour
2/3 cup beer
1 ½ teaspoons baking powder
¼ cup all-purpose flour
2 cups sweetened, flaked coconut (I generally use more as I really like to cake it on)
1 ½ pounds uncooked large shrimp, peeled and deveined with tails on
3 or so cups vegetable oil for frying

COMBINE the egg, the ½ cup flour, beer, and baking powder in a medium bowl. Place the remaining ¼ cup flour and coconut flakes in two separate bowls. Hold each shrimp by the tail and one by one dredge in the flour, then the batter, then the coconut; really patting the coconut on. Place each shrimp on a baking sheet lined with wax or parchment paper and chill in the refrigerator for at least an hour. Fry the shrimp in batches for 2 to 3 minutes over medium to high heat until golden brown. Serve with a sauce made of ¾ cup orange marmalade or apricot jam, ¼ cup Dijon style mustard, 2 tablespoons horseradish, and ¼ cup honey.

Fried Polenta Squares with Anchovy Sauce

Joel surprised me one Christmas by planning a bike trip for the two of us in Italy. Tuscany, to be exact. His gift to get me excited for our adventure was a beautiful cookbook full of the history of the area and endless mouthwatering recipes showcasing the foods we would soon be enjoying. Over the years I have created many of the dishes, but this is the one that everyone seems to like best. I serve it as a lead-in to many of my Italian dinners.

5 cups salted water
1 cup coarse-ground yellow polenta (cornmeal)
Vegetable or canola oil for frying

1/3 cup EVOO
1 garlic clove, minced
8 large olive oil-packed anchovies
2 tablespoons chopped, canned tomatoes
1 tablespoon capers, drained
1 teaspoon parsley, chopped
Coarse ground black pepper to taste

BRING the salted water to a boil in a deep saucepan. In a steady stream, pour in the polenta while stirring constantly. Reduce the heat to low and cook for about 30 minutes, stirring the polenta frequently. It is ready when the mixture becomes quite thick and pulls away from the pan as it is stirred. Remove from the heat and pour into a greased 9" by 12" baking pan. Smooth the polenta with a spatula or the back of a wooden spoon. Cover with plastic wrap and chill for several hours.

Meanwhile, make the sauce by warming the EVOO in a saucepan over low heat. Add the garlic and sauté about 1 minute. Stir in the anchovy fillets and break them apart in the pan with a wooden spoon. Cook for about 6 minutes or until the mixture thickens. Stir in the tomatoes, capers, and parsley. Season with pepper, then raise the temperature to medium and cook for another 10 minutes. Remove from the heat and set aside.

Invert the chilled polenta onto a cutting board and cut into 2 inch squares. Pour about 3 inches of vegetable or canola oil into a deep fry pan or skillet and heat to 350° degrees. Working in batches, fry the polenta squares, turning only once, for a total of about 10 minutes. They should be golden colored and crispy. Using a slotted spoon, transfer the squares to a wire rack to drain.

Arrange the polenta squares on a warmed serving platter and top each with a spoonful of sauce.

Garlic Escargots in Mushroom Caps

Coming from a large Italian family, Joel always enjoyed a 7 fish Christmas Eve celebration. When I took over the tradition several years ago, I changed things up and put my own twist on the menu. This dish is always a crowd pleaser.

1 (28 ounce) can of escargots, drained (I buy them on *Amazon*)
2 sticks unsalted butter
3 garlic cloves, minced
30 mushroom caps, stems removed
1 1/3 cups white wine
1 1/3 cups light cream
4 tablespoons all-purpose flour
Ground black pepper to taste
Salt to taste
1 tablespoon dried tarragon
1 cup grated Parmesan cheese

PLACE the escargots in a small bowl and cover them with water to remove any canned flavor they may have. Set aside for 5 minutes then drain and pat dry.

Preheat the oven to 350° and lightly grease a large baking dish.

Melt the butter with the garlic in a skillet over medium to high heat. Add the escargots and mushroom caps. Cook and stir until the mushroom caps begin to soften, about 5 minutes.

Whisk together the wine, cream, flour, pepper, salt, and tarragon in a small bowl. Pour into skillet and bring to a boil. Cook, stirring occasionally, until the sauce begins to thicken, about 12 minutes.

Remove the skillet from the heat and use a spoon to place the mushroom caps upside down in the prepared baking dish. Spoon an escargot into each mushroom cap. You may have more escargots than mushroom caps so just place them in the baking dish as well. Pour the remaining sauce over the mushroom caps and escargots. Sprinkle with the grated Parmesan cheese and bake at 350° for approximately 15 more minutes.

Seared Foie Gras with Cinnamon Raisin French Toast

I love foie gras! Anyone who knows me well is aware of my passion for this savory delight. To me there isn't anything more wonderful than a chilled glass of California chardonnay accompanied by a perfectly seared lobe of foie gras laced with a sweet sauce. Luckily, Joel feels the same way, so we order it out quite often. Or better yet, I prepare it at home. This is typically an appetizer, but we have been known to add a salad and call it dinner! Check out the "before" and "after" photos of a recently enjoyed foie gras on the front and back covers!

1 ½ pound lobe goose liver (I order online from *D'Artagnan*)

Salt to taste

4 slices of cinnamon raisin bread (I use my homemade bread, see Cinnamon Raisin Loaves)

2 eggs

¼ cup half and half

1 tablespoon sugar

1 teaspoon nutmeg

½ cup fruit preserve

Maple syrup to drizzle

WHISK the eggs, half and half, sugar, and nutmeg in a shallow bowl. Dip the cinnamon raisin bread slices in the egg mixture then cook in a buttered skillet until nicely browned on both sides. Cut into triangles or long strips and set aside but keep warm. Cut the lobe of foie gras into 1 inch slices and salt both sides. Heat a cast iron skillet on the stove (no need to use any grease as the lobes will produce enough!) and then sear the lobes over medium to high heat until they begin to shrink and create fat, turning only once. Quickly arrange the French toast pieces on a plate, then drizzle a little maple syrup over them. You can also spoon on any kind of warmed fruit preserve. Lay the lobes on top and enjoy. Be sure to turn off the stove before you rush off to eat. I forgot to do so one time, and we now refer to my singed ceiling as the unfortunate consequence of the foie gras incident!

Ground Pork and Vegetable Egg Rolls

In 2010, for our 25th wedding anniversary and Joel's 50th birthday, we embarked upon a spectacular adventure that included bicycles, a chase car, and 15 states along the United States eastern seaboard. We pedaled our way from Calais, Maine to Key West, Florida, leaving in the beginning of August and arriving at our destination in mid-October. My folks were always nearby in their "sag wagon" as we biked through all the major cities of the east coast, visiting family and friends whenever possible. Although we ate very well during the trip I found that I greatly missed my kitchen. When we had a wonderful 3-day layover in Williamsburg, Virginia with our friends Lisa and Michael, they sensed the one thing that I really wanted to do at this mid-point in our journey was cook. They whisked me off to the grocery store, lent me their kitchen, and let me do my thing. This is one of the dishes I made. For years I have fried these, but they are just as awesome when baked.

1 pound ground pork	2 cups carrots, shredded
1 small shallot, minced	2 cups snow peas, chopped
2 garlic cloves, minced	1 (15 ounce) can baby sweet corn (those cute little cobs), cut into slices
½ cup stir fry sauce	1 (9 ounce) jar ginger dressing
Salt and pepper to taste	1 (16 ounce) package egg roll wraps (20 wraps)
4 cups shitake mushrooms, chopped, stems removed	Canola oil for frying, olive oil for baking
4 cups red cabbage, shredded	Sweet and Sour sauce for dipping

WARM some canola oil in a skillet and sauté the minced shallot and garlic. Add in the ground pork, salt, and pepper and cook through. Remove to a large bowl with a slotted spoon. Mix in the stir fry sauce and set aside. Using the same skillet, cook the mushrooms until they soften. Remove and stir them into the meat mixture. In a separate bowl, mix together the cabbage, carrots, snow peas, and corn. Add some more canola oil to the skillet and cook the vegetable mixture for 3 to 4 minutes. Stir in the ginger dressing and some salt and pepper. Set aside. Wash the skillet, then begin to warm 3 inches or so of canola oil OR heat the oven to 400° and grease 2 baking sheets.

To prepare the egg rolls, (I always ask Joel to do this part!) lay one wrap on a cutting board and place a spoonful of both the meat and the vegetable mixtures in the center on a diagonal. Fold the bottom corner over the filling and roll snugly half way to cover the filling. Fold in both sides snugly against the filling. Moisten the edges of the last flap. Roll up and seal the top corner, then lay flap down until ready to cook. If frying, make sure the oil is up to 350°, and working in batches of 4 or 5 with the flap side down, fry the eggrolls for 2 to 3 minutes turning frequently to keep them evenly brown. Drain on paper towels until all are cooked. If you wish to bake them, place the egg rolls flap side down on the baking sheets and brush with olive oil. Bake at 400° for 10 to 12 minutes.

Horned Dorset Hot Cheese Dip

This has been a family favorite recipe for over 35 years. The Horned Dorset Restaurant in Leonardsville, NY has been our special occasion destination since it opened in the early 1980's. We have celebrated graduations, birthdays, anniversaries, and the like in style at this elegant establishment. They serve this dip as a complimentary starter, and it is delicious! They don't give out the recipe, so my brother and I played around a bit and finally hit upon a close approximation. This is my version.

1 cup real mayonnaise

2 cups sharp white cheddar cheese, shredded

1 yellow onion, finely chopped

Dash of Worcestershire sauce

COMBINE all ingredients in a bowl then transfer to a lightly greased large ramekin or casserole dish and bake at 450° until bubbly, about 15 minutes. Serve with *Ritz* crackers or crusty bread.

Pimento Cheese Dip

About 5 years ago, a special friend named Guylene came into my life. She hails from Montreal via Louisiana, and boy does she know how to cook! I have enjoyed learning from her as we spend many hours planning menus, shopping for ingredients, whipping up delicious meals for our husbands, families, and friends and just plain relishing our friendship and our kinship for amazing food. This is a southern staple that Guylene introduced me to. She adds many more ingredients, but I have chosen to stick to this simple yet crowd-pleasing version.

1 cup sharp yellow cheddar cheese, shredded
1 cup pepper jack cheese, shredded
1 (4 ounce) brick cream cheese, softened a bit

3 to 4 tablespoons pimentos, drained
Salt and pepper to taste
¼ cup real mayonnaise

PLACE the three cheeses in a large mixing bowl and begin to blend with a hand mixer. Add in the pimentos, salt, pepper and mayonnaise and continue to blend until creamy. Can be served right away with club crackers or chilled and saved for a later time.

Guacamole, Salsa Style

I first learned how to make guacamole back in college. A friend taught me and I was hooked, but little did I know that simply adding salt and garlic powder to mashed avocadoes does not even come close to what a true guacamole dip can be! My friend Mitch's flavorful dish opened my eyes to all the fun ingredients you can toss in to create this wonderfully fresh and healthy snack. My recipe is just right for 8 friends to share. Adjust the ingredients as you wish to feed more or less.

4 ripe avocados
1 large garlic clove, chopped
3 tablespoons fresh cilantro, chopped
3 tablespoons red onion, minced
1 cup salsa from a jar, medium to hot, based on your taste
¼ cup black beans, drained
Juice of ½ lime
Salt and pepper to taste

PEEL and mash the avocados in a large mixing bowl. Stir in the remaining ingredients. Serve immediately with blue corn chips or any tortilla chip of your liking.

Rumaki (Bacon Wrapped Chicken Livers)

When I was a kid, I remember my parents throwing lively cocktail parties. My brother and I would get in our pajamas and hide on the top step of the staircase to watch all the revelry from above. This was a favorite appetizer of the times. It remains popular in our home today. I also do a seafood version of this recipe by swapping out the chicken livers for the small, sweet scallops that I buy from John at his fish truck when he comes to town every Thursday afternoon.

Bacon
1 (20 ounce) container chicken livers
Coarse ground black pepper

PREHEAT the oven to 400°.

Spread strips of bacon on a parchment lined baking sheet. Sprinkle with coarse ground pepper. Cook in the oven for 10 to 13 minutes, or until almost done but still pliable, not crispy. Cool slightly.

Drain the chicken livers. Cut each liver in half or at least into bite-size portions. Place a liver at one end of a strip of bacon, then roll up and insert a toothpick to hold together. Turn on the broiler. Place the tray on a rack a few inches below the broiler and cook, watching the entire time so they do not burn. In 5 to 7 minutes you will be ready to enjoy.

Shrimp Creole Appetizer

For several years Joel and I were lucky enough to be part of a fun gourmet club. There were five couples and we rotated houses with the hosts determining the menu and distributing the recipes. This savory starter is from Brenda. I serve it often!

1 ½ pounds raw shrimp, peeled and deveined

2 or 3 slices uncooked bacon

1 ½ sticks unsalted butter

2 tablespoons Dijon style mustard

½ teaspoon dried basil

¼ teaspoon dried thyme

1 teaspoon black pepper

½ teaspoon dried oregano

2 fresh garlic cloves, chopped

3 tablespoons *Old Bay* seasoning

1 teaspoon hot sauce (feel free to use more if you like heat!)

PLACE the raw shrimp into a baking dish.

Preheat the oven to 350°.

Cut the bacon into smallish bits, then fry them in a heavy skillet. Drain off some of the fat and add all of the above ingredients to the bacon and cook over medium heat until bubbly and fragrant. Pour this sauce over the shrimp and stir to combine.

Bake for 20 minutes, stirring halfway through.

Serve in individual bowls with crusty bread on the side for dipping.

Notes

Soups, Salads, and Sandwiches

Chicken Noodle Soup

Pear and Leek Soup

Creamy Clam Chowder

Butternut Squash Soup Laced with Lime and Ginger

Hearty Vegetable and Pasta Soup

Caesar Salad

Classic Wedge Salad with Blue Cheese Dressing

Strawberry and Spinach Salad

Arugula Salad with Beets and Fried Goat Cheese

Watermelon, Feta, and Mint Salad

Turkey and Cheese Sandwich Wraps

Monte Cristo Sandwiches

Tuna Melt

Apple and Brie Paninis

Notes

Chicken Noodle Soup

This is an intuitive dish. I don't think I have ever followed a recipe. I make it regularly, and it always comes out tasting just the same, delicious. Oh, and it really does help cure the common cold. Trust me on this one!

Split whole chicken, approximately 3 pounds
EVOO
2 garlic cloves, minced
1 medium onion, chopped
5 carrots, peeled and sliced
3 celery stalks, sliced
Salt and pepper to taste
2 cups chicken stock
1 (12 ounce) bag extra wide egg noodles
Fresh parsley
Shredded Parmesan cheese

BRING 8 cups of salted water to a boil in a soup pot. Add the chicken and simmer for about 20 minutes. Remove the chicken and place on a wooden cutting board with a well to catch the juices. Set aside to cool. Strain the water, return it to the pot, and keep it warm on the stove. Meanwhile, heat the EVOO in a skillet and sauté the garlic, onion, carrots, and celery until soft but not browned. Season with the salt and pepper. Add the sautéed vegetables along with the 2 cups of chicken stock to the pot of strained water. Simmer. Remove the skin from the cooled chicken and cut the meat into bite-size pieces. Add to the soup. Boil the egg noodles according to the package instructions, drain, and add to the soup. Add more salt and pepper if needed. Continue to simmer for about 10 minutes to allow the flavors to mingle, then ladle into bowls and garnish with parsley and Parmesan cheese.

Pear and Leek Soup

Kelly, my friend from our gourmet club, asked me to bring this soup to her dinner party. I was very pleased with how easy it was to make, and at the same time how rich and delicious it turned out. This is a keeper. I still make it frequently, usually during the winter months, and I always get excited when I do because I can utilize the cool immersion blender that Joel got me for Christmas several years ago!

1/3 cup sweet butter
3 cups leeks, washed well and sliced
4 pears, peeled, cored, and coarsely chopped
6 cups chicken stock
1 teaspoon ground savory
¼ teaspoon white pepper
1 tablespoon fresh lemon juice
1 pear, peeled, cored, and thinly sliced
Crumbled blue cheese

HEAT the butter in a large soup pot. Add in the leeks and sauté until softened but not browned, about 10 minutes. Stir in the chopped pears, chicken stock, savory, and pepper. Bring to a boil then reduce the heat and simmer until the pears are softened. Stir in the lemon juice. Using an immersion blender, run until smooth. Serve warm, garnished with the pear slices and blue cheese.

Creamy Clam Chowder

I have always loved to vacation in New England. One time upon returning home from a weekend trip to Cape Cod, I got inspired to prepare a coastal meal and invited my parents over to share it with us. I made this chowder and Susan's blueberry bread and a cob salad. I remember my dad asking me if this was all we were having. I was confused until he declared that he wanted a second bowl because it was so good, but he didn't want to fill up if there were more courses! The addition of sweet potatoes came a little while back when I made it for our 7 fish Christmas Eve dinner and wanted to give it a little color.

3 dozen littleneck clams, rinsed
1 lemon, cut into wedges
Old Bay seasoning
6 slices uncooked bacon, diced
3 tablespoons salted butter
1 cup onion, chopped
½ cup celery, chopped
1 ½ cups water
2 cups white potatoes, cubed
2 cups sweet potatoes, cubed
½ cup corn, fresh if possible
3 cups half and half
Salt and pepper to taste
Fresh rosemary and thyme, chopped

BRING 3 cups of water to a boil in a large, shallow pot. Add the clams, lemon wedges, and *Old Bay*. Cover and cook until the clams have opened, about 8 minutes. Remove the clams from their shells and set aside.

Cook the bacon in a large soup pot over medium to low heat until almost crisp. Add in the butter, onions, and celery and cook for about 5 minutes. Stir in the water and both types of potatoes and season with salt and pepper. Bring to a boil and let cook for about 15 minutes. Check the potatoes with a fork to make sure they are soft. Add in the corn. Stir and let rest on very low heat for a few minutes. Add in the clams and the half and half. Cook for about 5 more minutes. Sprinkle in a mixture of the rosemary and thyme to taste and stir to combine.

Butternut Squash Soup Laced with Lime and Ginger

One autumn day many years ago, my friend Pam and her family joined us on a leaf peeping trip which included a tour of some underground caverns and a delicious lunch at a little café in the middle of practically nowhere. We had the tastiest squash and apple soup. We couldn't stop raving about it! We both tried our hand at mimicking it over the coming years. While playing around with different combinations of flavors, I came up with this version. I began to serve it at our annual end-of-summer dinner party at Sylvan Beach because it is easy to double or even triple to feed large crowds.

1 cup onion, finely chopped

3 or 4 tablespoons unsalted butter

2 cups water

2 cups chicken stock

4 cups butternut squash, cubed

3 garlic cloves, minced

2 to 3 tablespoons freshly squeezed lime juice

Salt and pepper to taste

Vegetable or canola oil

Ginger root, peeled and cut into slivers

MELT the butter in a soup pot and add the onion. Cook until softened. Add in the water, chicken stock, cubed squash, and garlic. Bring to a boil. Reduce the heat to medium and simmer until the squash is soft, about 20 minutes. Add in the lime juice as well as the salt and pepper. Using an immersion blender, run until the soup is smooth. Meanwhile, fry up the slivers of ginger root in a skillet with the oil until crispy. Drain on a paper towel. Sprinkle on top of each serving.

Hearty Vegetable and Pasta Soup

While Christmas shopping one year, Joel spied a table full of bargain-priced cookbooks and bought me one that boasted of 50 ways to cook pasta. What fun I have had making my way through the recipes. This soup is delicious. It can be served as a light lunch, or add a salad, some crusty bread, and a cheese plate and it makes a lovely supper.

1 onion, chopped

1 garlic clove, minced

1 large leek, washed and sliced

1 tablespoon EVOO

2 medium carrots, sliced

1 (14 ounce) can chopped or diced tomatoes

5 cups vegetable stock

2 medium green and/or yellow zucchini squash, sliced

1 cup cabbage, shredded

½ cup green beans, ends trimmed and halved

½ cup uncooked elbow macaroni

Salt and pepper to taste

SOFTEN the onion, garlic, and leek slices in a large soup pot with the EVOO. Add in the carrots, tomatoes, and vegetable stock. Bring to a boil, then cover and simmer for 30 minutes. Stir in the zucchini, cabbage, beans, and macaroni and season with salt and pepper. Continue to simmer until the macaroni is cooked, about 10 to 15 minutes.

Caesar Salad

For years I was in awe of a great Caesar salad. I would order it out but never attempt to make it at home. Perhaps it had something to do with the fear of raw eggs. A few years ago, another of my good friends from our gourmet club, Maria, gave me her recipe which used partially cooked eggs. I tested it out and was pleased with the results. Not long ago, Maria called to ask if I still had her recipe as she could not find it and wanted to make it for her dinner guests. Coincidentally, I was making it that same day for our own guests. Thank goodness for texting technology because within minutes her request was filled. It almost felt like we were cooking together!

salad

2 heads Romaine lettuce, washed and torn
4 garlic cloves, finely chopped
1 tablespoon anchovy paste
½ teaspoon salt
2 teaspoons fresh lemon juice
1 teaspoon Worcestershire sauce
½ cup EVOO
2 coddled eggs (boiled in their shells for 2 minutes)
½ cup Parmesan cheese, shredded
1 (2 ounce) tin flat anchovies

croutons

2 tablespoons butter
2 tablespoons EVOO
2 garlic cloves, halved
3 cups ½ inch bread cubes
salt and pepper to taste

MELT the butter with the EVOO and garlic cloves in a small saucepan. Remove from the heat and let sit for 10 minutes. Extract the garlic. Add salt and pepper. Toss over the bread cubes and spread on a baking sheet. Bake at 350° until golden brown.

For the salad, mix the garlic, anchovy paste, and salt in a wooden salad bowl. Whisk in the lemon juice and the Worcestershire sauce. Add the EVOO in a slow, steady stream, stirring constantly. Crack the eggs and whisk them in until blended. Toss in the Romaine and the croutons. Sprinkle the Parmesan cheese on top. Offer anchovy fillets on the side as an accompaniment.

Classic Wedge Salad with Blue Cheese Dressing

For a while I got stuck in the 90's when this salad appeared on many restaurant menus. I'm glad I hung in there, though, because it seems to be making a resurgence. I love it as an accompaniment to a grilled steak or a hearty pasta dish. The dressing is especially delicious!

salad

1 head iceberg lettuce

1 ripe tomato, chopped into very small bits

1 English cucumber, chopped into very small bits

1 small red onion, chopped, also into very small bits

3 or 4 strips of crisp bacon, crumbled

3 ounces crumbled blue cheese

Salt and pepper to taste

dressing

2/3 cup sour cream

½ cup mayonnaise

¼ cup buttermilk

1 garlic clove, minced

juice of ½ a lemon

MAKE the dressing by mixing the sour cream, mayonnaise, buttermilk, garlic, and lemon juice in a bowl. Season with salt and pepper and stir in the blue cheese. Chop the lettuce into desired amount of wedges. Top with tomatoes, cucumbers, and onions, then drizzle with the dressing and the bacon bits.

Strawberry and Spinach Salad

This one is as simple as it sounds. I can't even count the number of times I have served this at luncheons and showers as well as summer dinner parties. It also works well for just Joel and me if I halve the recipe.

2 bunches fresh spinach, washed and patted dry
1 pint fresh strawberries, sliced
½ cup sugar
1 tablespoon poppy seeds
2 tablespoons sesame seeds
2 teaspoons minced onions
½ teaspoon paprika
½ cup vegetable oil
¼ cup cider vinegar
Dash of Worcestershire sauce

MIX the spinach and the berries together in a large bowl. Whisk the dressing ingredients together and pour over the salad. Toss and enjoy.

Arugula Salad with Beets and Fried Goat Cheese

When I was growing up I truly disliked beets. Luckily, my palate matured and I have discovered interesting ways to cook and enjoy them on their own as well as added into other dishes. This recipe combines the sharp, peppery taste of arugula with the sweetness of beets and adds some soft, warm goat cheese and crunchy seeds on top. Well, let's just say this is a wonderful salad.

1 package arugula

1 cup beets, roasted and diced

1 (11 ounce) log goat cheese

Panko crumbs

Pinch of cayenne pepper

2 egg whites,

1 tablespoon water

¼ cup EVOO plus extra for cooking the goat cheese

1 tablespoon unsalted butter

1 tablespoon champagne vinegar

2 teaspoons Dijon style mustard

1 garlic clove, minced

2 teaspoons red onion, finely diced

Salt and coarse ground black pepper to taste

Toasted, shelled sunflower seeds

PREPARE the beets ahead of time by scrubbing them, cutting off the tops and bottoms, and drizzling them with some EVOO, salt, and pepper. Wrap them loosely in aluminum foil. Bake in a 350° oven for at least an hour. Once they have cooled, the skins will peel right off and you can dice as much as needed.

To make the dressing, mix the ¼ cup EVOO, vinegar, mustard, garlic, red onion, salt, and pepper in a cruet or jar. Shake to blend. Use a strip of dental floss to cut ½ inch slices of the goat cheese. Place the panko in a shallow bowl and season with the cayenne pepper. Whisk the egg whites with the water in another shallow bowl. Dredge each goat cheese slice in the egg whites, then coat with panko. Set on a baking sheet and chill for 15 to 20 minutes. Melt the butter and 1 tablespoon of EVOO in a skillet. Over medium to high heat, fry the goat cheese quickly. They are done when brown on both sides but no cheese is melting out. Toss the arugula with the dressing, sprinkle the desired amount of diced beets on top, lay on a couple slices of goat cheese and top with the sunflower seeds.

Watermelon, Feta, and Mint Salad

Credit for this refreshing summer salad goes to Joel's cousin Carol. Back when Joel Rhein was in college, we purchased a rundown house near his campus and spent the better part of a year travelling to Saratoga to renovate it for his eventual occupancy. Carol and her husband Bob happened to live right across the street and put us up until we could actually stay at the house. Not only did they both help us with the remodel, but Carol also fed us wonderful meals. This dish became a favorite of mine.

½ watermelon, cut into bite-size chunks
3/4 cup feta cheese, crumbled
2 tablespoons fresh mint, chopped
Honey for drizzling

MIX the watermelon, feta, and mint together in a decorative serving bowl. Drizzle with some honey. Serve and enjoy.

Turkey and Cheese Sandwich Wraps

About 10 years ago I got hooked on sandwich wraps. I believed, perhaps erroneously, that I could still enjoy a delicious sandwich without the calories of bread. I experimented with spinach, sundried tomato, and wheat tortillas, as well as plain old flour wraps. My mom has come to love them as well, but only the way I make them! When I switched from using just mayonnaise to a garlic aioli spread, the pleasure just increased.

wraps
1 (10 ounce) package flour tortillas
Alfalfa sprouts
Avocado slices
Tomato slices
Deli turkey slices
Swiss cheese slices
Slices of cooked, crisp bacon

aioli
1 cup mayonnaise
3 garlic cloves, minced
1 tablespoon fresh lemon juice
Pinch of cayenne pepper

MAKE the aioli by whisking together the mayonnaise, garlic, lemon juice, and cayenne pepper in a bowl. Cover and chill to let the flavors mingle. When ready to assemble, place the wraps on a cutting board and spread the aioli on them all the way to the edges. Lay down several slices of turkey in the center of the wrap followed by the cheese and some bacon. Cover with the sprouts, tomatoes, then the avocados last. Fold in the right and left sides, then roll the wrap and its fillings away from you. Cut in half and enjoy with some chips.

Monte Cristo Sandwiches

Sometimes I feel like an old soul. I love the nostalgia of the past; especially the food. This sandwich seems to have evolved over the years from a French dish called a Croque Monsieur. I remember enjoying Monte Cristo sandwiches all throughout my childhood during the 1960's and 1970's, which makes sense because this version of the European original became popular in the United States in the late 1950's.

Sourdough bread, crusts trimmed off
Smoked turkey breast slices
Honey baked ham slices
Provolone cheese, sliced
Swiss cheese, sliced
Mayonnaise
Dijon style mustard
2 eggs, lightly beaten
Light cream
Butter
Maple syrup
Powdered sugar

ASSEMBLE the sandwiches by spreading mayonnaise on one slice of bread and mustard on the other. Lay slices of turkey, then provolone on the mayonnaise side. Lay some Swiss, then the ham on the mustard side. Combine the 2 sides and compress. Wrap tightly in plastic wrap and refrigerate. When you are ready to cook them, dip in a mixture of the eggs and cream. Melt some butter in a skillet and gently place the sandwiches in. Cook, turning only once, until both sides are golden and the cheese is soft and melted. Serve in quarters drizzled with maple syrup. Sprinkle some powdered sugar on top.

Tuna Melt

Lunch is my favorite meal of the day. I sometimes skip breakfast (not too smart I realize) and I savor dinner, but I really look forward to that mid-day repast. Since the kids have gone off and started their own lives and I have tapered back on work, I am often home alone during the noon hour. I enjoy preparing a meal for myself, complete with a place setting and perhaps some jazz on the radio. Tuna melts are my go-to sandwich. I change up how I make them, but the basic recipe is as follows.

Sliced whole wheat or multigrain bread
½ pound very fresh tuna steak,
approximately 1 inch thick
1 celery stalk, finely diced
2 tablespoons red onion, finely diced
2 tablespoons mayonnaise
2 teaspoons spicy mustard
EVOO
Salt and pepper to taste
A dash of garlic powder
Sliced Swiss or sharp cheddar cheese
Kosher Dill pickle, sliced lengthwise

RUB the tuna steak on both sides with some EVOO and sprinkle on some salt, pepper, and garlic powder. Coat a stove top grill pan with cooking spray. Sear the tuna on medium to high heat for about 10 minutes. Remove and let cool. Chop the tuna into small chunks and place in a bowl. Mix in the vegetables, mayonnaise, mustard, and some salt and pepper. Lay a slice of cheese on a slice of bread, then slather with about half of the tuna mixture and top with another slice of cheese, the sliced pickles, and the other slice of bread. Melt some butter in a skillet and slowly cook the sandwich over low to medium heat until it is brown on both sides and the cheese is oozing out. Save the remainder of the tuna and enjoy with crackers as a late day snack!

Apple and Brie Paninis

I do not own a panini press, but these sandwiches are almost better when you warm them in a buttered skillet. You can make them with individual ciabatta rolls or use a large focaccia bread cut into quarters.

12 slices Applewood smoked bacon
1 large Golden Delicious Apple, unpeeled but cored and thinly sliced
Dijon style mustard
1 (16 ounce) wedge Brie cheese, rind trimmed off and cut into slices
Ciabatta rolls or large focaccia bread
3 tablespoons butter, divided

COOK the bacon in a skillet until crisp. Remove and drain on paper towels. Melt 1 tablespoon of the butter in another skillet and add in the apple slices. Sauté for about 4 minutes. Remove and set aside. Wash the skillet to reuse for the sandwiches. Spread the mustard on the cut side of whichever bread you choose. Place 2 slices of cheese on each mustard covered bottom piece, then top with 4 to 5 apple slices and 3 bacon slices. Top each with more cheese. Cover with the top slice of bread and press the sandwich together. Melt the remaining butter over medium heat in the skillet and place in 2 sandwiches. Cover the skillet and cook until the bottoms are brown, pressing with a spatula to compact. Turn the sandwiches over, cover, and cook about 5 more minutes. Repeat with the remaining sandwiches.

Notes

Real Deal Main Meals

Tuna Tartare

White Chili

Broccoli Hats

Salmon in Puff Pastry

Spinach and 4 Cheese Stuffed Chicken Breasts

Dad's Mouth Watering Meatballs

Creamy, Cheesy Shrimp and Grits

Lamb Shepherd's Pie

Cracker Crusted Fried Haddock

Veal Cordon Bleu

Sausage and Peppers Calzone

Seafood Lasagna

Chicken and Asparagus Burritos

Chicken Riggies

Double Stuffed Cheeseburgers

Buttermilk Fried Chicken

Notes

Tuna Tartare

Ever since John, the fish truck guy, has been coming to Rome once a week, I have been experimenting more and more with seafood recipes. I usually have a meal in mind before I get to the truck, but sometimes he is sold out of what I want or something else strikes my fancy and I go off on a tangent. I often buy tuna, then decide what to do with it once I get home. Last summer, some friends, Bob and Cindy, stopped over late in the day to check out the decorative grasses in our garden as they were creating a new backyard space. One thing led to another, which led to drinks, then an invitation to stay for dinner. Cindy helped me put together this tartare on the fly, as I had just been to visit John and had a beautiful piece of tuna ready to be enjoyed.

1 pound very fresh tuna steak
¼ cup EVOO
2 tablespoons capers
2 tablespoons red onion, minced
1 tablespoon parsley, chopped
Juice of ½ a lime
Salt and pepper to taste
Dash of hot sauce
Mixed field greens
Goat or feta cheese, crumbled

CUT the tuna into ¼ inch cubed pieces and place in a large mixing bowl. Stir in the EVOO, capers, red onion, parsley, and lime juice. Season with the salt, pepper, and hot sauce. Mix well, then spoon into small ramekins. Chill for 30 minutes. Toss the field greens with some EVOO, salt and pepper and place on salad plates. Invert the tuna on top and sprinkle with either goat cheese crumbles or feta crumbles.

White Chili

There are so many different ways to make chili. I do like the ground beef, kidney bean, red sauce version, but lately it has been fun to experiment with white meats and white beans. This recipe uses shredded turkey breasts. I even bought white pepper to stay true to the theme! Chili is great any time of year, although it seems to taste best on cold, blustery autumn evenings as the wind howls and the leaves twist and twirl. Think Halloween...

2 turkey tenderloins, approximately 1 ½ pounds meat

EVOO

1 onion, chopped

2 garlic cloves, minced

3 cups turkey stock

1 (4 ounce) can chopped green chili peppers

2 (14 ounce) cans cannellini beans, undrained

1 teaspoon chili powder

1 teaspoon cayenne pepper

1 teaspoon *Louisiana Cajun* seasoning

1 cup shredded Monterey Jack cheese

BOIL the tenderloins for about 10 minutes in a large pot of salted water. Add in some EVOO and white pepper as well. Remove the meat and set aside on a wooden cutting board to cool. Heat some EVOO in a large skillet and sauté the onion and garlic until soft. Add in the turkey stock, chopped green chili peppers, and the spices. Bring to a boil. Shred the turkey and add into the pot along with the beans. Reduce the heat to low and simmer for 25 minutes, or until thickened and heated through. Adjust the seasonings and serve in individual bowls with the shredded cheese on top.

Broccoli Hats

The interesting back story to this recipe is that, like oral history, I learned how to make it from a conversation, and I have continued to share it verbally...until now! Way back when our sons were toddlers, my friend Cathy and I would meet at the playground midway between our houses and chat while the boys dug in the sandbox. In addition to solving all the world's problems, we often talked about food and what we were making for dinner that night. This is Cathy's recipe, and I have followed her instructions faithfully for over 25 years.

1 head broccoli, cut into florets
2 garlic cloves, minced
3 ½ cups chicken stock
1 pound orecchiette pasta (hats)
EVOO
Salt and pepper to taste
Fontina cheese

SAUTÉ the garlic in a skillet with some EVOO for just a few minutes. Add in the broccoli florets and sauté until almost soft, about 5 to 6 minutes. Season with salt and pepper. Pour in the chicken stock and bring to a boil. Lower the temperature and simmer. Meanwhile, cook the pasta according to the package instructions. When the pasta reaches the desired doneness, drain and return to the pot. Pour in the broccoli and chicken stock mixture. Stir to combine. Serve in individual bowls and grate some fresh Fontina cheese on top.

Salmon in Puff Pastry

Whenever I plan a dinner party I try to prepare most of the dishes ahead of time so that I can enjoy the evening and my guests and not be too tied up in the kitchen. This recipe is perfect because you can assemble the puffs beforehand and cook them while you serve appetizers and drinks. The flavors, colors, and textures, all nestled inside the warm, flaky pastry are quite delicious!

4 salmon fillets, skins removed
2 sheets puff pastry, thawed
Bunch of leeks, washed and sliced
2 medium onions, sliced
1 (8 ounce) brick dill Havarti cheese, shredded
EVOO
½ stick unsalted butter
Salt and pepper to taste
1 egg
1 tablespoon water
Balsamic glaze

CARAMELIZE the leeks and onions in a skillet with the EVOO and butter. Cook long enough to get some brown bits. Season lightly with salt and pepper. Set aside. Roll out the 2 sheets of puff pastry on a lightly floured board and cut each in half. Rub each salmon fillet with EVOO and season with salt and pepper. Place about ¼ cup of shredded Havarti cheese on each puff. Top with ¼ cup caramelized leeks and onions. Finally, lay a salmon fillet across the mixture. Whisk the egg and water together to make a wash then brush the edges of the pastry and fold up all sides. Press to seal. Place the four puffs, seam side down, on a parchment lined baking sheet and brush the tops with the egg wash. Bake in a 350° oven for approximately 30 minutes. Drizzle with some balsamic glaze before serving.

Spinach and 4 Cheese Stuffed Chicken Breasts

This is a wonderful dinner party offering. It is easy to prepare and can be assembled the night before. I recall serving it at our new home on Turin Road before we had even moved in. My kitchen was installed, and the dining room table and chairs had been set up, so I figured why not invite 8 friends over to help christen the new digs? The only thing I had not anticipated was the Indian summer-like evening that caused us all to curse the heat and lack of air conditioning. At least the food was good! Oh, and we still do not have AC...

4 large chicken breasts
1 cup whole milk ricotta cheese
½ cup Parmesan cheese, grated
¾ cup gouda cheese, shredded
¾ cup sharp cheddar cheese, shredded
1 cup fresh spinach, chopped
Garlic powder
Salt and fresh ground black pepper to taste
EVOO

CUT a wide slice in each chicken breast and pull back the meat to create a hollow cavity. Rub some EVOO over each breast to coat entirely, inside and out, then season with garlic powder, salt, and pepper. Make the stuffing by mixing the ricotta, Parmesan, gouda, cheddar, and spinach in a large bowl. Season with garlic powder, salt, and pepper. Using your hands, place a quarter of the stuffing into each chicken breast cavity. Place into a lightly greased baking dish and cook in a 350° oven for 25 minutes.

Dad's Mouth Watering Meatballs

Any cook can get frustrated when their loved ones or guests snatch up some yummy item that they are preparing faster than they can keep up. It is best, though, to plan for this happy phenomenon and make more than enough to go around. Also, try to relish the compliments and join in the fun! My dad's meatballs are the best ever and warrant stealing while cooking. As kids, my brother and I loved Sunday afternoons when Dad would fry these lovelies up. We would hover in the kitchen, grabbing the meatballs as they came out of the skillet, often filling up before the spaghetti dinner main event. My dad taught me his secret recipe years ago, and I have been making it ever since with the very same gentle, hand-slapping fun.

10 large eggs
1 tablespoon garlic salt
1 tablespoon onion salt
½ teaspoon coarse ground black pepper
1 teaspoon or more parsley and basil
1 cup grated Parmesan cheese
1 or more cups *Ritz* cracker crumbs
1 ½ -2 pounds ground beef
½ -1 pound Italian sausage
EVOO and safflower oil for frying

WHISK the eggs in a large bowl and mix in the garlic salt, onion salt, pepper, parsley, and basil. Knead in the meats, Parmesan cheese, and cracker crumbs. Add some water if needed to keep it moist. Roll about 2 tablespoons of the mixture in the palms of your hands to form balls. Heat some EVOO and safflower oil about ½ inch deep in a skillet and fry the meatballs in batches until brown all over.

Creamy, Cheesy Shrimp and Grits

Grits are not on everyone's list of favorite foods, but I sure like them. I was introduced to them as a breakfast side when we were house hunting in the Carolinas years ago. I still order them with my morning meal when we are down south, but I love them even more as a dinner entrée. There are so many ways to prepare a delicious shrimp and grits dish, and I have tried several different variations. It always tastes best, though, coming out of my Emerald Isle kitchen because I can get the shrimp fresh from our local fishmonger that same day. I order the Tasso ham online from D'Artagnan. Oh, and if you add a fried egg or two on top of the leftovers the next morning, you have yourself one terrific breakfast.

1 cup stone ground yellow grits

3 cups water

1 teaspoon salt

2 cups half and half or light cream

2 to 3 pounds uncooked shrimp, peeled and deveined

Salt and pepper to taste

Pinch of cayenne pepper

EVOO

1 cup Tasso ham, diced

1 green pepper, chopped

1 red pepper, chopped

1 onion, chopped

1 garlic clove, chopped

¼ cup butter

¼ cup all-purpose flour

1 cup chicken stock

Dash of hot sauce

1 cup sharp cheddar cheese, shredded

½ cup green onions (scallions), chopped

BRING the water, salt, and grits to a boil in a heavy saucepan. Stir in the cream and simmer until the grits are tender, about 15 minutes. Cover and set aside. Heat some oil in a heavy skillet and sauté the ham until crisp, about 8 minutes. Remove from the skillet and set aside. Sauté the vegetables and garlic in the Tasso drippings for about 8 minutes or until soft. Sprinkle the shrimp with some salt and the cayenne pepper and add to the vegetable mixture in the skillet. Cook for only about 30 seconds or until the shrimp just turns pink. In a saucepan, melt the butter then add in the flour and stir over medium heat until it forms a nice brown paste, about 6 minutes. Add the paste into the skillet with the shrimp and vegetables then pour in the chicken stock and add in the Tasso ham. Throw in a dash of hot sauce and a little salt and pepper. Simmer over medium heat until the sauce thickens, about 6 minutes. Meanwhile, add the shredded cheddar into the warm grits and stir to mix well. Serve the shrimp, vegetable, and ham mixture over the cheesy grits. Sprinkle with chopped scallions.

Lamb Shepherd's Pie

Sometimes I choose to cook something just so that I can use one of my jazzy kitchen tools. I bought a ricer (food mill) a few years back and keep forgetting that it is still in the box stored down in the basement. As autumn approaches each year, I yearn for hearty fall one-dish meals like this shepherd's pie. Even though it can be prepared without a ricer, it is lots more fun to dig it out and give it a whirl.

5 medium to large Yukon gold (yellow) potatoes, peeled, and chopped

3 tablespoons unsalted butter, softened

1/3 cup light cream

1 egg, beaten

3 tablespoons EVOO

Salt and pepper to taste

2 teaspoons dried rosemary

1 ¾ pound ground lamb

3 garlic cloves, minced

1 medium onion, chopped

5 medium carrots, peeled and chopped

1 cup corn, fresh if possible

½ cup red wine, plus 2 tablespoons

2 cups chicken stock

2 tablespoons cornstarch

2 teaspoons Worcestershire sauce

½ cup Parmesan cheese

PREPARE the potatoes by adding them to a large pot of salted, cool water and bringing them to a boil. Reduce the heat and simmer until tender, about 12 minutes. Drain the potatoes in a colander for a few minutes to allow them to dry. Push the potatoes through a ricer into a large mixing bowl. Add in the butter, cream, egg, and 1 tablespoon of the EVOO. Stir until well mixed and very smooth. Set aside. Heat the remaining 2 tablespoons EVOO in an ovenproof skillet and cook the lamb, stirring occasionally, until browned. Season with salt, pepper, and rosemary. Remove to a bowl and set aside. In the same skillet, sauté the garlic, onions, and carrots until softened, about 8 or so minutes. Stir in the corn. Add the lamb back in and stir to mix well. Pour in the ½ cup of red wine and cook for a few minutes. Add in the chicken stock and the Worcestershire sauce and bring to a boil. Meanwhile, combine the remaining 2 tablespoons of red wine with the cornstarch and stir into the lamb and vegetable mixture. Simmer until a thick gravy has formed. Remove from the heat and top with the potatoes. Sprinkle on the Parmesan cheese. Cook under a broiler for 5 minutes, or until the potatoes become a beautiful brown. Serve immediately.

Cracker Crusted Fried Haddock

Fish fries seem to be a tradition in upstate New York, especially on Fridays during Lent. When the kids were young, we had fun scouting out different places that served them. Joel Rhein and Paige may deny this now, but the only time we ever saw them fight or disagree was when we were at a restaurant and one or the other would order the fish fry, then the other would get upset and not order it because they had gotten beaten to the punch! So, I decided to start making them at home to keep the peace. Sure, it stunk up the house for a while, but the results were pretty darn good.

fish
4 haddock fillets, skins off
1 cup all-purpose flour
Salt and pepper to taste
2 tablespoons *Old Bay* seasoning
2 sleeves *Ritz* crackers, crumbled
2 eggs
Vegetable or canola oil for frying

tartar sauce
1 cup mayonnaise
1 tablespoon sweet pickle relish
1 tablespoon lemon juice
salt and pepper to taste

MIX the flour with the salt, pepper, and *Old Bay* in a shallow bowl. In a different bowl, whisk the eggs with some water. Place the cracker crumbs in a third bowl. Add the oil into a heavy skillet until it reaches about halfway up the sides. Heat to 300°. Dredge the haddock fillets in the flour, then dip into the egg mixture, and finally pat on the cracker crumbs to entirely cover the fish. Fry in batches, trying not to turn too many times, until done, about 3 minutes. Using 2 spatulas helps to keep the fish from breaking in the middle. Serve with homemade tartar sauce.

Veal Cordon Bleu

This recipe goes back to my new bride days. I had invited some fellow Hamilton alums over for dinner when we lived in Philadelphia, and I wanted to do something special...well at least above and beyond my usual ham steaks and baked chicken. The meal was a success, and I have reproduced the recipe many times, often jazzing it up a bit with a béchamel sauce or a fruit chutney topping.

4 boneless veal cutlets

4 thin slices deli ham

4 thin slices Swiss cheese

2 tablespoons all-purpose flour

½ teaspoon salt

½ teaspoon pepper

¼ teaspoon allspice

1 egg, slightly beaten

½ cup dry bread crumbs

6 tablespoons shortening (really, I wrote that! use butter)

PLACE the veal between 2 pieces of wax paper and pound to tenderize. Layer each cutlet with cheese and ham, then roll up and fasten with toothpicks. Combine the flour, salt, pepper, and allspice in a shallow bowl. Dredge each cutlet in the flour mixture. Next, dip in the egg, and finally coat with the bread crumbs. Chill, uncovered, in the refrigerator for at least two hours. This will help the coating to stay on during the cooking phase. When ready to cook, melt the butter in a skillet and cook the cutlets over medium heat for 20 to 25 minutes, turning frequently to keep them from burning.

Sausage and Peppers Calzone

Sometimes a certain dish reminds me of a special person or couple. Whenever I make these calzones, I think of our friends Joanne and Nick. When Joanne's step-father passed away many years ago, I delivered a few of these to their home, hot and ready for family members to nibble on during those first few hours after the funeral. As time passed, I continued to prepare them whenever we were invited out on their boat for an afternoon cruise because they pack up so well and are easy to cut and serve. This past Christmas, I invited Nick and Joanne over for holiday cocktails and snacks. Of course calzones were on the menu! As with many of my dishes, the ingredients can be mixed and matched or changed up in so many enjoyable ways. I have made vegetarian calzones with whatever produce is fresh or in season. They are also delicious with chicken, broccoli, and cheddar cheese. Experiment. Have fun.

1 ball pizza dough (I use my homemade dough, see Breakfast Pizza)
1 large onion, sliced
1 pound bulk sausage, sweet or medium
3 medium peppers (red, green, yellow), julienned
1 ½ cups mozzarella cheese, shredded
Parmesan cheese
EVOO
Butter
Salt, pepper, garlic powder

BEGIN by caramelizing the onions. Sauté the slices in a skillet with just enough EVOO to cover the bottom and about ¼ stick of butter. They are done when they turn a deep, rich color, and brown bits begin to form. Set aside.

Preheat the oven to 350° and begin to warm a pizza stone. Let the dough come to room temperature while you brown the sausage in a skillet. Remove the sausage, then soften the peppers in the skillet, adding in the caramelized onions at the end. Roll out the dough on a cutting board to an 8" by 16" rectangle. Rub all over with EVOO and season with salt, pepper, and garlic powder. Layer, first by spreading the shredded mozzarella, then the sausage, and finally the peppers and onions. Sprinkle with Parmesan cheese. Fold up the sides and the ends and place, seam side down, on a pizza peel dusted with cornmeal. Push onto the heated pizza stone and cook for 30 to 35 minutes.

Seafood Lasagna

The origins of this recipe elude me. I know I first came up with it as a Christmas Eve offering long before I began doing the 7 fish dinner, and it has definitely become the star of that gathering. Also, it has endured many transformations as I experimented with different fish and a variety of cheeses. No matter how it is put together, though, it is well liked. This is the first time that I have actually written down the ingredients, measurements, and steps. Usually I just wing it!

lasagna
½ stick butter
Salt and pepper to taste
Old Bay seasoning
1 shallot, minced
4 garlic cloves, minced
1 pound salmon, skinned and chopped
1 pound raw shrimp, peeled and chopped
1 pound scallops
2 cups ricotta cheese

1 egg
½ cup Parmesan cheese
¼ cup parsley, chopped
16 ounces Muenster cheese, shredded
Lasagna noodles

white sauce
1 stick butter
½ cup all-purpose flour
4 cups milk
Parmesan cheese

MAKE the white sauce first. In a saucepan, melt the butter over moderately low heat. Stir in the flour and cook the roux for about 3 minutes. Add the milk in a steady stream and bring the mixture to a boil, whisking until thick and smooth. Add salt and pepper to taste and simmer over low heat, whisking occasionally until thickened. Let cool a bit and stir in some Parmesan cheese. Cover with plastic wrap and set aside. Prepare the cheese mixture next by mixing the ricotta with the egg, Parmesan cheese, some salt and pepper, and the parsley. Season the scallops with salt, pepper, and *Old Bay*. Melt half of the butter in a skillet and sear the scallops until brown on both sides. Remove and set aside. Add the rest of the butter to the same skillet and stir in the shallots and garlic. Sauté for a few minutes, then add in the shrimp and salmon. Cook for 5 to 7 minutes. Chop the scallops and add back into the skillet with the other fish. Stir all together and let simmer for a few minutes. The salmon may break up a bit.

Meanwhile, boil the pasta according to the directions on the box. Drain. Now the fun begins… spread some white sauce in the bottom of a 9" by 13" baking dish. Place down 3 noodles. Top with dollops of the ricotta mixture and spread to entirely cover the pasta. Using a slotted spoon, layer on the fish. Top with a handful of shredded Muenster cheese. Repeat 2 more times layering first the noodles, then the white sauce, then the ricotta, then the fish, then some cheese. End with white sauce, shredded Muenster, and some Parmesan cheese as the top layer. Bake in a 350° oven for 35 to 40 minutes.

Chicken and Asparagus Burritos

This tasty dish is loaded with lots of good stuff. It is one of those meals that you can open your refrigerator and get creative with what is on hand. I like to make this for large crowds because it is filling and delicious, and I can do it all ahead of time. Years before we were invited to join the gourmet club, we enjoyed the company of 4 other couples and called ourselves the Go-Out-to-Dinner-Club. We each hosted a few dinners at our homes, but for the most part we liked piling into 2 or 3 cars and exploring area restaurants. When one of our group was moving to Florida, I offered to cook for everyone, kids included, as a farewell party. This is what I made, and it was a hit. As written, it serves 2 or 3, so adjust accordingly.

6 slices bacon

½ pound chicken breast, cut into thin strips

2 garlic cloves, minced

1 ½ cups salsa from a jar

1 (15 ounce) can cannelloni beans, undrained

1 small green pepper, chopped

1 small red pepper, chopped

¼ cup scallions, chopped

1 bunch asparagus, blanched in vegetable stock

1 cup Monterey Jack cheese, shredded

½ teaspoon cumin

¼ teaspoon chili powder

Salt and pepper to taste

½ cup light cream

6 flour tortillas

Vegetable or canola oil for frying

COOK the bacon in a skillet until crisp. Remove, crumble, and set aside. Reserve 1 tablespoon of the bacon fat and cook the chicken and garlic until both are tender but not quite done. Add in ½ cup of the salsa, beans, peppers, cumin, and chili powder. Season with salt and pepper. Simmer for 7 or 8 minutes until thickened, stirring occasionally. Stir in the scallions and bacon. Let the flavors mingle for a few minutes while you flash fry each tortilla in a skillet with very hot oil to crisp them up. Do not overcook as you want the tortillas to remain pliable. Assemble the burritos one at a time by layering them first with the chicken and bean mixture, then a few stalks of asparagus, and finally with some cheese. Roll up and place in a greased baking dish, seam side down. Combine the remaining salsa with the cream and spread over the top. Bake at 350° for 15 or so minutes. Remove from the oven and sprinkle some cheese over all the tortillas. Cook for 5 more minutes.

Chicken Riggies

Most people from outside of Central New York are unfamiliar with chicken riggies. It is somewhat of a regional dish originating in the Utica/Rome area. Many local restaurants serve it in various forms, and there is an annual competitive cook-off to determine who does it best. Several years ago, my friend, Heidi, found a riggie recipe in our hometown newspaper and shared it with the girls in our coffee group. We all took off with it and began to make it our own. Mine became popular with Paige and her high school friends and carried on into college. She routinely brought her Syracuse Rugby team home for a chicken riggie fix. I found myself doubling and tripling the recipe to keep up. I also took the recipe on the road, so to speak, when I hauled pots, pans, and utensils up to Maine where Joel Rhein was studying medicine and couldn't get home for his birthday. We invited 20 or so of his classmates over for riggies and birthday cake. Fun times all around!

10 tablespoons margarine (not butter)
1 medium onion, chopped
4 hot cherry peppers from a jar, chopped
2 garlic cloves, chopped
1 tablespoon parsley, chopped
Salt and pepper to taste
1 pound chicken breast, cut into chunks
Flour for dusting
¼ cup sherry
½ cup heavy cream
½ cup tomato sauce
½ pound rigatoni pasta
Grated Parmesan cheese

PLACE the onion, cherry peppers, and garlic in a food processor and coarsely chop. Melt the butter in a heavy skillet, and add in the onion mixture. Sauté over low heat for 4 to 5 minutes. Dredge the chicken pieces in flour and add to the pot. Cook slowly over medium heat until done, stirring frequently so the chicken doesn't stick to the bottom of the pan. Add in the sherry, heavy cream, and tomato sauce and season with the salt, pepper, and parsley. Let simmer for a bit. Meanwhile, cook the rigatoni following the package directions. Drain and add to chicken mixture. Stir, making sure all the pasta gets covered with sauce. Sprinkle with Parmesan cheese and serve with crusty bread and a fresh green salad.

Double Stuffed Cheeseburgers

It is probably fairly obvious that most of my recipes have an accompanying story. This one is no different except that the circumstances surrounding it could have been much better. Joel and I, along with my brother and his wife, treated my parents to a 40th wedding anniversary gift of a week's vacation all together on Nantucket Island in August of 1999. We packed up the kids, our bikes, some beach toys, and the grandparents and headed for paradise. Only Chris could make it, as Susan was pregnant with their twins and didn't want to risk the travel. In any event, the week was spectacular. We ate in. We dined out. We discovered all the neat things that Nantucket has to offer. All was good until the last day when Joel took the kids into the wildly rough ocean for one last swim. I paced the shore nervously until he sent one child to me, then the other. He started to body surf in himself when a rogue wave slammed him face-first onto the ocean floor, flipping his legs over his head, breaking a vertebra in his neck. Long story short, Joel was airlifted off the island while my parents and I scurried to pack up, load the vehicle, try to remain calm and think about what to serve for dinner because after all, the kids were still little and had to eat, right? Dad fashioned these burgers together, and I will always remember how good they tasted despite the fact that we were all beside ourselves with worry for Joel. He did fine, thank goodness, and we were able to reunite with him just outside of Boston. Mom's college roommate, Sandy, saved the day by picking him up at the hospital, keeping him overnight, then driving him to meet us at a rest stop on the Massachusetts Turnpike. Lengthy tale…great burgers. This recipe makes 2 burgers. Adjust the ingredients as needed to make more.

Approximately 1½ pounds grass fed or angus ground beef
½ medium onion, finely chopped
½ cup shredded cheddar cheese

¼ cup crumbled blue cheese
Garlic powder
Salt and pepper to taste

SEASON the meat with the garlic powder, salt, and pepper. Divide into four equal portions and flatten into patties. Layer two of the patties with onions, cheddar and blue cheese. With moistened hands, top with the other patties and close the seams, working the two halves into one beautiful burger. Cover and chill until ready to grill. Cook to the desired amount of doneness and serve with lettuce, tomatoes, and bacon on homemade buns.

For the buns, refer back to Cinnamon Raisin Loaves. Use 3 cups warm water, omit the buttermilk, and instead of using cinnamon and raisins and placing the dough into a loaf pans, make 6 buns from roughly ½ pound of the chilled dough. Brush the buns with olive oil, season with some sesame seeds, and bake in a 400° oven for 20 or so minutes.

Buttermilk Fried Chicken

Wow, is this ever good!! I think it has become my signature dish, although I have had lots of help perfecting it along the way. It started out as a bon appétit *recipe, but over time I have adjusted the seasonings and experimented with different methods of frying. Guylene bought a propane fueled deep fryer a few years back after I told her I was going to make fried chicken for a party of 30 or so people. She was concerned that my stovetop skillet plan was going to take way too long. What a production! What fun! The chicken turned out beautifully. It was so good, in fact, that we decided to take the fryer down to Emerald Isle the next year and cook for Paige and her friends. Half the fun of this meal is the group participation and preparation. Our friend, Charlie, is especially good at rubbing the chicken with the spice mixture, and Paige is a pro at dredging it in the buttermilk and flour. No one fries it better than Guylene, though. Sometimes it takes a crowd to make a party. Even though Joel Rhein has not yet pitched in on a fried chicken cook-off, he proclaims it to be "mad" good and once ate 5 pieces in a sitting!*

4 tablespoons Kosher salt

2 tablespoons coarse ground black pepper

1 tablespoon garlic powder

1 tablespoon paprika

1 tablespoon Cayenne pepper

2 pounds chicken thighs, drumsticks, and breasts (10 pieces total)

1 cup buttermilk

½ cup water

1 egg

3 cups all-purpose flour

1 tablespoon cornstarch

Vegetable or canola oil for frying

MIX the spices in a shallow dish like a pie plate. Dredge each piece of chicken in the mixture and rub the spices in well. Place the rubbed chicken in a 13" by 9" glass dish, cover with plastic wrap, and chill overnight. When you are ready to cook, bring a skillet full of oil (or use a deep fryer outside!) to 325°. Whisk the buttermilk and the egg with the water in a medium bowl. Sift the cornstarch into the flour in another medium bowl. Dunk each piece of chicken first into the buttermilk mixture then into the flour mixture. Working in batches, fry the chicken pieces, turning occasionally until they turn a beautiful golden brown, about 10 minutes per batch. Breasts may take a little longer. Serve with honey and hot sauce.

Notes

Veggie and Starchy Sides

Multi-Color Coleslaw

Mustard Glazed Carrots

Brussel Sprouts

Maple Spiced Sweet Potatoes

Spinach Casserole

Roasted Asparagus

Tempura Fried Vegetables

Cauliflower Gratin with Goat Cheese and Gnocchi

Mushroom Risotto

Duck Fat Fries with Parmesan Cheese and Truffle Oil

Notes

Multi-Color Coleslaw

My mom makes a really good coleslaw. She uses her mother's recipe and tweaks it a bit. A fond memory I have of this dish is when Mom got Pam's youngest child, Aidan, to help her make it at the Outer Banks house during one vacation. Our two families rented at the beach during the school spring break for over 12 years. As the kids got older and began inviting friends, and Pam and I started including our parents and siblings, the dinner table sometimes grew to 20 or more hungry people. That meant everyone was asked to pitch in and help with either the grocery shopping, table setting, cooking, or cleaning up. No one seemed to mind. The teacher and student's coleslaw was delicious! I have taken the recipe and put my own twist on it. It adds a tasty crunch to a picnic-style meal.

3 cups red cabbage, chopped
½ cup plain Greek yogurt
¾ cup mayonnaise
1 tablespoon apple cider vinegar
1 Granny Smith apple, cut into small chunks
½ cup golden raisins
¼ cup California raisins
Sea salt
Coarse ground black pepper

MIX the yogurt and mayonnaise together in a medium bowl. Stir in the cabbage. Add the cider vinegar, apples, and raisins. Season with salt and pepper. Chill for at least an hour before serving.

Mustard Glazed Carrots

My recipe collection was fairly limited when I was a newlywed, but I was determined to try out new dishes to impress Joel and to throw frequent dinner parties for his colleagues and our new friends in Philadelphia. This is one of those early test kitchen attempts that I still make today, usually in the spring. As is evident, this is nothing fancy, but it does add color to a ham or pork roast dinner.

1 (16 ounce) bag baby cut carrots

1 teaspoon salt

3 tablespoons butter

3 tablespoons prepared mustard, spicy brown or honey Dijon

¼ cup packed brown sugar

¼ cup chopped parsley

Salt and pepper to taste

BOIL the carrots in a saucepan of salted water for about 10 minutes or until just tender. Drain and place in a casserole dish. Cook the butter, mustard, and brown sugar in a saucepan until syrupy, about 3 minutes. Pour over the carrots and season with salt and pepper. Stir to coat. Cook at 400° until bubbly, about 15 minutes. Sprinkle with parsley and serve immediately.

Brussel Sprouts

This recipe has taken on a life of its own. There does not seem to be a right or wrong way to prepare Brussel sprouts, but certainly some variations are tastier than others. I have tried boiling and steaming them, but even when heavily seasoned they seemed boring. Then I began to par-cook and broil them, but I was not ecstatic with the outcome. Sautéing seems to be the answer!

1 ½ pounds Brussel sprouts, washed, ends cut off, and cut lengthwise into quarters

1 (4 ounce) package diced pancetta

2 tablespoons EVOO

3 tablespoons butter

½ cup Parmesan cheese, shredded

COAT a skillet with the EVOO and brown the diced pancetta for 3 to 4 minutes. Remove and set aside. Add more oil to the pan as well as the butter. Add in the Brussel sprouts and stir until all the leaves are coated. Caramelize over low to medium heat, stirring frequently to keep from burning, about 10 to 12 minutes. When nearly done, add the pancetta back in and season with salt and pepper. Sprinkle with the shredded Parmesan cheese and serve right away.

Maple Spiced Sweet Potatoes

There is no real story to accompany this side dish except to say that it is very flavorful. It adds that seasonal touch to an autumn meal. The crème fraiche really tempers the spice.

sweet potatoes

2 large sweet potatoes

¼ pound sweet cream butter

3 tablespoons real maple syrup

1 teaspoon *Tony Chachere's Creole Spice*

crème fraiche

2 cups heavy cream

2 tablespoons freshly squeezed lemon juice

MAKE the crème fraiche ahead of time. Mix the heavy cream and the lemon juice in a mason jar. Cover and let sit for 8 to 10 hours at room temperature. Refrigerate. The mixture will become very thick.

Bake the sweet potatoes in a 350° oven for approximately 1 hour. Let cool a bit, then remove the skins and place the potatoes in a large mixing bowl. Add in the butter, maple syrup, and creole spice. Beat with a hand mixer until very smooth and light. Serve hot with a dollop of crème fraiche.

Spinach Casserole

When our kids were little, Pam and I were always searching for ways to get them to eat their vegetables. She tried this one out on her gang of 4 and shared the recipe with me.

3 eggs

2 tablespoons all-purpose flour

1 bag frozen spinach, defrosted and drained

4 ounces cottage cheese

6 ounces shredded cheddar cheese

Parmesan cheese

PREHEAT the oven to 350°. Beat the eggs and flour together, then stir in the spinach and cheeses. Pour into a pie plate or an 8" square baking pan, sprinkle on some Parmesan cheese, and bake for 30 minutes or until bubbly and brown.

Roasted Asparagus

I recall eating asparagus from a can when I was young and thinking to myself "there must be a better way to enjoy this squishy, soggy green food." As I now know, fresh is always best, and roasting is an easy way to prepare almost any vegetable.

2 bunches fresh asparagus
2 tablespoons EVOO
½ teaspoon sea salt
Coarse ground black pepper
Shaved Parmesan cheese

PREPARE a baking sheet by drizzling the EVOO and salt and pepper on it and smearing it around. Place trimmed asparagus stalks on the seasoned oil and roll them around until well coated. Place in a 400° oven and roast for about 10 minutes. You will need to shake the pan midway through to make sure the asparagus cooks evenly. Serve immediately with some Parmesan cheese sprinkled on top.

Tempura Fried Vegetables

These wonderful tidbits can accompany an Italian meal just as easily as an Asian-inspired one. Merely change up the vegetables and offer different dipping sauces and you are good to go.

1 cup all-purpose flour
Pinch of salt plus salt to taste
2 egg yolks, lightly beaten
½ cup white wine
½ cup water
1 red pepper, cut into 8 pieces
1 head broccoli, cut into florets
10 or so large mushroom caps
Vegetable or canola oil for frying

POUR the flour into a large bowl and form a well in the middle with your fingers. Sprinkle a pinch of salt in the well and then add in the egg yolks and the wine. Blend together with a wooden spoon. Add in the water and whisk until smooth but not runny. Chill for at least an hour. Bring the oil up to 350° degrees in a heavy skillet, making sure that it is 4 to 5 inches up the sides. Dredge the vegetables in the batter and gently drop into the oil. Working in batches, cook until brown, about 3 to 4 minutes. Use a slotted spoon to remove to a serving platter. Sprinkle with salt and serve immediately.

Cauliflower Gratin with Goat Cheese and Gnocchi

This recipe had a fun evolution. It began with Kelly asking me to make it for a gourmet club dinner. I followed her recipe and everyone was pleased. I then began to prepare it for our family gatherings and also when we entertained friends. Once, when Guylene was over, she mentioned that she used gnocchis in her version. I started to do that, as well as add in goat cheese and switch from using prosciutto to bacon. The bottom line is this dish is pretty delicious any way we gals prepare it! Proof of its popularity came last Easter when my niece, Emily, specifically requested that I make it for the family dinner.

1 head cauliflower, cut into florets

8 to 10 slices bacon, diced

6 tablespoons butter

4 garlic cloves, minced

2 tablespoons all-purpose flour

1 ½ cups heavy cream

1 ½ cups grated Swiss cheese, plus more for topping

1 (4 ounce) log goat cheese, cut into small pieces

Pinch of cayenne pepper

Salt and pepper to taste

PREHEAT the oven to 350°. Fry the diced bacon in a skillet until almost crispy. Remove and set aside. Pour off most of the bacon fat, then add in the butter and garlic and sauté about 2 minutes. Mix in the cauliflower and cook until it begins to lose its crispness, about 4 to 5 minutes. Stir in the flour and then the cream. Blend well. Season with the cayenne pepper, salt, and pepper. Heat to almost boiling, then add in the Swiss and goat cheeses, allowing them to melt. Add the bacon bits back in. Pour the cauliflower mixture into a shallow au gratin dish, sprinkle with some more Swiss cheese, and bake for approximately 30 minutes.

Mushroom Risotto

I don't quite remember when I discovered that I absolutely love risotto, but I think it might have been when we stumbled upon a back alley Italian restaurant in Boston's Back Bay area. Joel had their osso buco, and I tried something new. Well, at least for me. Delicious! I did not attempt to make it at home right away because people told me how hard it is to get just right. It wasn't until my dad gave me the Intercourses *cookbook with this recipe in it that I found out how wrong they all are. I have played with many different add-ins but keep coming back to just mushrooms.*

1 ½ tablespoons unsalted butter
½ teaspoon EVOO
Salt and pepper to taste
1 small onion, diced
¾ cup Arborio rice
2 cups chicken stock, heated
1 pound mushrooms, sliced
¼ cup heavy cream
Parmesan cheese

MELT the butter in a large skillet and sauté the onions until tender. Stir in the rice and cook for 1 minute. Add in the hot chicken stock all at once. This is when people told me that the stock had to be ladled in slowly over 30 to 40 minutes. My way works. Believe me! Season with salt and pepper. Cook, uncovered, over low heat, stirring frequently until the rice is tender on the outside and chewy on the inside. Meanwhile in another saucepan, sauté the mushrooms in the EVOO. When the rice is done, fold in the mushrooms, heavy cream, and Parmesan cheese. Sprinkle some more Parmesan cheese on top before serving.

Duck Fat Fries with Parmesan Cheese and Truffle Oil

Did I make your mouth water with the name alone? These are truly decadent. I love them. Enough said? Since duck fat is not a staple at our local upstate New York grocery stores, I rely on Guylene to keep me well stocked whenever she comes to visit. She now lives a few miles from the Canadian border and zips up there often for her meats, cheeses, and other delicacies. I was recently talking food with my friend Bob who renders his own fat from ducks he orders online and cooks up with his son for family gatherings. We plan to team up soon to prepare a duck-themed French feast at my house. Can't wait!

4 medium potatoes (russet work best)
8 cups vegetable or canola oil
2 cups duck fat
Sea salt
Coarse ground black pepper
Truffle oil or essence
Parmesan cheese, grated
Fresh parsley, chopped

PEEL the potatoes and cut them into thin matchsticks. Place them into a bowl of cool water and let sit for an hour to get the starchiness out of them. Drain and pat dry with paper towels, then carefully add into the oil which should be heated in a deep skillet to a temperature of 325°. Work in batches and cook for about 5 or 6 minutes, or until the potatoes just start to change color. Drain on paper towels. Meanwhile, heat the duck fat in a heavy saucepan. Make sure to get the temperature up to around 375°. Cook the fries until brown and crispy. Again, drain on paper towels. Lastly, arrange the potatoes on a baking sheet. Sprinkle with the sea salt and pepper and drizzle with the truffle oil. Grate some fresh Parmesan cheese over the top. Place in a 400° oven for just a few minutes. Serve immediately with fresh parsley tossed on top.

Notes

Sweet Endings

Pineapple Coconut Cake

Molten Chocolate Lava Cakes

Lemon Tart

Ice Cream Cookie Sandwiches

Chocolate Mint Brownies

Very Vanilla Cheesecake

Carrot Cake

Profiteroles (Cream Puffs)

Peach Crisp

Nana's Better-than-Sex Cake

Notes

Pineapple Coconut Cake

My roommate from college, Randi, would often invite me to her home on Long Island during our school breaks. I loved those trips because we got to explore New York City, visit the north and south shores of the Island, and enjoy Randi's mother's cooking. This dessert was a favorite of mine, and I was quite pleased when she shared her recipe. Recently I have been making it for the sweets case at Kikko's. It is best served warm with homemade whipped cream.

½ cup butter
1 cup sugar
1 unbeaten egg
1 cup undrained, crushed pineapple
1 teaspoon vanilla extract
1 ½ cups sifted flour
1 teaspoon baking soda
1 teaspoon salt
½ cup sweetened, flaked coconut
½ cup packed brown sugar

CREAM together the butter and sugar. Add in the egg, crushed pineapple, and vanilla. Stir in the flour, soda, and salt. Spread into a greased 8" square baking pan. Mix the coconut flakes and brown sugar together and sprinkle on top. Bake in a 350° oven for 40 minutes.

Molten Chocolate Lava Cakes

I learned how to make these heavenly cakes after enjoying the ones that our chef at La Mariposa made for our dinner guests. I thought they would be hard to perfect, like a mousse, but was surprised to find out how easy this recipe is. Although they are pleasing at any time of year, I especially like to share them with loved ones on Valentine's Day with red berries and a dollop of fresh whipped cream.

1 stick unsalted butter

1 (6 ounce) bar of bittersweet chocolate, chopped

2 large eggs

2 large egg yolks (save the whites for an omelet!)

¼ cup sugar

Pinch of salt

2 tablespoons all-purpose flour

PREHEAT the oven to 450°. Grease 4 medium-sized ramekins. In a double boiler, melt the butter with the chocolate. In a medium bowl, beat the sugar, eggs, egg yolks, and salt until pale and thickened. Whisk the chocolate mixture until smooth, then quickly fold into the egg mixture. Whisk in the flour. Spoon the mixture into the ramekins. Set on a baking sheet and bake for 11 minutes. Run a knife around the edges after cooling for 1 minute, then invert onto plates. Adorn and serve.

Lemon Tart

Joel's brother Jeff just loves these. Every year he gives up desserts for Lent, and he admits that this treat tests his willpower. The shortbread crust teamed with the tart lemon filling is just so good!

1 cup all-purpose flour
½ cup unsalted butter, softened
¼ cup powdered sugar
2 eggs
1 cup granulated sugar
½ teaspoon baking powder
¼ teaspoon salt
2 tablespoons fresh lemon juice

MIX the flour, butter, and powdered sugar together. Press evenly into an ungreased 8" square baking dish or round tart pan. Bake at 350° for 20 minutes. Beat the remaining ingredients for about 3 minutes, or until light and fluffy. Pour over the hot crust. Bake for 25 minutes longer, or until no imprint remains when touched lightly. Cool, cut, and serve.

Ice Cream Cookie Sandwiches

Okay, these are not exactly a rocket science dessert, but they sure are good, and everyone enjoys them during the summer months while lounging by the pool! I use the Toll House chocolate chip cookie recipe from the bag and a high quality vanilla bean ice cream. Make a full batch of cookies. Try to get them all about 2 to 3 inches in diameter. Allow them to cool completely. Lay the cookies out upside down on a cutting board. Using an ice cream scooper and your hands, squash little balls of ice cream into patties and press between two cookies. Wrap each cookie sandwich individually in wax paper and place them all in a large zip lock bag. Store in the freezer in an easily accessible space so that when the overwhelming urge hits for this summertime treat, you won't waste any time searching for them!

Chocolate Mint Brownies

This dessert is a Christmas tradition. Joel Rhein and Paige still ask for it when they come home for the holidays. We used to live in a neighborhood where everyone was over-the-fence friends. The kids and I would deliver a little plate of these brownies to the folks next door and across the street as December 25th drew near. We were always invited in for a visit and perhaps a mug of hot chocolate. I went to make them again last year and discovered that my recipe card had smeared. I couldn't read the ingredients for the middle layer! I called my mom, as I was sure she held the secret recipe. No such luck. So I went onto the internet and cobbled together a couple of different recipes to recreate the original. I think I got it right.

brownies

1 cup sugar

½ cup soft butter

4 eggs

1 cup all-purpose flour

½ teaspoon salt

1 (16 ounce) can chocolate syrup

1 teaspoon vanilla extract

mint layer

2 cups powdered sugar

½ cup butter, softened

¼ cup *crème de menthe* liquor

topping

1 cup chocolate chips

6 tablespoons butter

MIX together the ingredients for the brownies and place in a greased 13" by 9" pan. Bake in a 350° oven for 30 minutes. Cool thoroughly. Combine the powdered sugar, butter, and *crème de menthe*. Spread over the brownies. Refrigerate for at least half an hour. Melt the chocolate chips and the butter in a saucepan. Stir until smooth, then spread evenly over the cooled mint layer. Refrigerate for an hour before cutting into squares.

Very Vanilla Cheesecake

It seems like I have been making cheesecakes forever. My first was, of course, a New York style with strawberries on top. I then got hooked on variations of pumpkin. I began to experiment with other flavors and made them as gifts for holidays or if people needed a special dessert for a party or event. Most recently my brother-in-law, Tom, has given me a dessert venue at his wine bar and bistro. I work there on occasion and provide weekly cheesecakes. This one seems to be an overwhelming favorite! Even though vanilla beans are quite pricey, they definitely take this cheesecake over the top.

1 package vanilla *Oreo* sandwich cookies

¼ cup unsalted butter, melted

4 (8 ounce) bricks cream cheese, room temperature

1 ½ cups sugar

5 eggs

2 vanilla beans, split lengthwise, seeds scraped out

1 tablespoon real vanilla extract

¾ cup sour cream

½ cup heavy cream

PLACE the cookies into a large plastic bag and crush them with a rolling pin. Mix the cookies in a bowl with the melted butter and press into a 10" springform pan that has greased parchment paper fastened into the bottom. Set aside. Beat the cream cheese and sugar for at least 3 minutes, then begin adding the eggs one at a time. Keep beating until smooth. Add the vanilla bean seeds, vanilla extract, sour cream, and heavy cream and beat 1 more minute. Cook at 300° for approximately 1 hour and 20 minutes. When the cheesecake is done, allow it to cool down inside the oven with the door open. Chill overnight if possible. Serve with homemade vanilla-flavored whipped cream.

Carrot Cake

This is one of those desserts that you almost always have the ingredients already on hand. It is so easy to make and is very moist and delicious. I use my friend Tracey's recipe for cream cheese frosting on top as it is a perfect complement to this decadent cake. Also, since Paige bought me a beautiful new bundt pan for Christmas, it has a much prettier presentation!

cake
2 cups sugar

1 ¼ cups vegetable or canola oil

4 eggs

3 cups carrots, grated

2 cups all-purpose flour

1 teaspoon salt

½ teaspoon baking soda

2 teaspoons cinnamon

frosting
1 (8 ounce) brick cream cheese, softened

½ stick butter, room temperature

2 cups powdered sugar

2 teaspoons vanilla extract

MIX together the sugar, oil, and eggs in a large bowl. Stir in the flour, salt, baking soda, and cinnamon. Fold in the grated carrots. Pour into a greased bundt pan and bake in a 350° oven for 1 hour. To make the frosting, beat the cream cheese and butter. Add in the powdered sugar, then the vanilla last. Mix well.

Profiteroles (Cream Puffs)

Before I took on the 7 fish family gathering, I would cook a lovely dinner for my parents and Nana starting around 6 pm on Christmas Eve. We would have hors d'oeuvres while the kids opened one present each and Joel Rhein read the Twas the Night Before Christmas story. I looked forward to this party, and I began to get fancy and try to experiment with new dishes. My mom has always loved profiteroles for dessert, so I learned how to make them. They quickly became a part of our holiday tradition. A fun twist is that for the filling I use Grandma Minnie's pudding recipe which my niece, Sarah, wrote out for me when she was just a child. Sarah is all grown up and married now and is a great cook.

cream puffs

½ cup water

¼ cup margarine

½ cup all-purpose flour

2 eggs

pudding

¼ cup sugar

5 tablespoons cornstarch

2 cups milk

1 egg, beaten

1 teaspoon vanilla extract

caramel sauce

3/4 cup sugar

¼ cup water

1 cup heavy cream

½ stick unsalted butter

Dash of salt

1 teaspoon vanilla extract

MAKE the pudding ahead of time. Combine the sugar and cornstarch in a saucepan. Stir in the milk gradually. Cook over medium heat, stirring constantly until the mixture thickens and boils. Boil and stir for at least 1 minute. Remove from the heat and pour half of the mixture into a bowl with the beaten egg. Return the egg and batter mixture back to the saucepan and boil and stir for 1 more minute. Remove from the heat and stir in the vanilla. Place plastic wrap over the pudding and chill.

For the cream puffs, heat the water and margarine to a rolling boil in a saucepan. Stir in the flour. Stirring vigorously over low heat, wait for the mixture to form into a ball and remove from the heat. Beat in the 2 eggs until smooth. Heat the oven to 400°. Drop the batter onto an ungreased baking sheet and bake for 35 minutes. Once they have cooled, gently cut off the tops and fill with the pudding. Sprinkle with powdered sugar or drizzle with homemade caramel sauce, or both! Makes 6 medium profiteroles.

Put the water and sugar in a heavy saucepan and bring to a boil. Do not stir! When it turns a deep brown color and starts to smoke, remove from the heat and stir in the cream, butter, salt, and vanilla.

Peach Crisp

This is an easy dessert that I make all year round. I just substitute whatever fruit is in season for the peaches. I was making it so frequently a few years ago that Joel asked me to slow down a bit as he did not want to gain weight. I think his exact words were "lead me not into temptation!"

3 cups fresh sliced peaches, skins on
2 tablespoons lemon juice
2/3 cup packed brown sugar
½ cup all-purpose flour
½ cup quick-cooking oats
1/3 cup unsalted butter, softened
¾ teaspoon cinnamon
¼ teaspoon salt

ARRANGE the peach slices in an ungreased 8" square baking dish. Spritz with the lemon juice. Mix the brown sugar, flour, oats, butter, cinnamon and salt. Sprinkle on top of the fruit and bake for about 30 minutes in a 375° oven.

Nana's Better-than-Sex Cake

Oh, the giggles we had with this one over the years! Even though Nana was a fine lady, she had a fun, mischievous side. She liked to serve this cake to her women friends and have a great laugh over its name. Nana handwrote this recipe for me as a bridal shower gift along with her many other favorites. I made it once for our gourmet club if only to start a lively discussion on whether it was true or not.

1 box yellow cake mix
1 (4 ounce) bar sweet German chocolate, shredded
1 box instant vanilla pudding
½ cup vegetable or canola oil
½ cup water
3 eggs
1 (6 ounce) package chocolate chips

MIX all of the above ingredients together. Pour into a greased bundt pan and bake at 350° for 45 to 55 minutes. Test the middle with a toothpick to be sure it is cooked through. Easy. Delicious!

Acknowledgements

First and foremost, I would like to heartily thank my friend and photographer, Karen Barnes, for bringing my recipes to full-color life on the pages of this book. Karen is an extremely talented artist with an eye for design and a real feel for nuance and ambiance. We had so much fun during our lunchtime photo shoots! The weeks of organizing and planning, shopping and cooking, testing and tasting all came together in seamless harmony each afternoon that we met to work on my project. We also had several dinner sessions which included our husbands, candles, and music. All gatherings ended in a substantial meal and lots of leftovers.

I would also like to recognize the influence that John and Diane Macpherson of the Foster Harris House in Washington, Virginia had on my decision to launch into this endeavor. Joel and I spent our anniversary weekend with the Macphersons last fall as part of a bicycle trip called Tour d'Epicure. We were so looking forward to this combination of gourmet food, cycling, and a stay at a quaint bed and breakfast that we rallied on, even after torrential autumn rains forced Diane to cancel the trip. We were the only brave souls to show up anyway, and we were royally treated to John's amazing fare and Diane's gracious flair for innkeeping. We even snuck in a bike ride between rain drops. Joel purchased their cookbook for me upon our departure, and I read through it word for word on our long drive home. The seeds of inspiration had been planted! Diane was kind enough to answer all sorts of questions about their publishing experience in the months that followed, and subsequently I found myself on the LifeRich path with my very own cookbook in print.

Resources

No matter how much a chef creates on his or her own, there are always guides and templates to help them along. I refer to the following books, magazines, and internet sites on a regular basis to confirm my measurements and procedures as well as get my culinary ideas flowing and my specialty kitchen items ordered.

Betty Crocker's Cookbook, Golden Press/New York, Tenth Printing, 1983

Joy of Cooking, Irma Rombauer and Marion Rombauer Becker, the Bobbs-Merrill Company, 1984

Intercourses, an aphrodisiac cookbook, Martha Hopkins and Randall Lockridge, Terrace Pub., 1997

bon appétit Magazine, Food & Wine Magazine, Coastal Living Magazine

allrecipes, Food Network, Epicurious, Amazon, D'Artagnan

About the Author

There isn't a food that Holly Amidon doesn't like to eat, or cook! A native of upstate New York, she has travelled extensively, sampling dishes from around the globe, but finds herself most at home with the comfort foods of her youth. Using fresh ingredients and recipes steeped in tradition, Holly creates meals that are meant to be shared. She loves to cook for family and friends, but has also forayed into the restaurant world at various times of her life. Whether it is an intimate dinner for two or a party for fifty, Holly's food makes people happy.

CPSIA information can be obtained
at www.ICGtesting.com
Printed in the USA
BVOW05s0148031116
466783BV00016B/174/P